Living Cruelty 1
compassion. _... ...

By Jennifer Thomson

ISBN-13: 978-1503081987
ISBN-10: 1503081982

Cover image courtesy of © Zcello | Dreamstime.com - White Rabbit Photo

Acknowledgements

I would like to thank the following for their invaluable help with this book:

My partner John, who helped me with the picture research, and who acted as a soundboard for content ideas.

My fellow tweeters on Twitter who helped clarify in my mind what needed to be included in this book.

My friends on Facebook who also helped me decide on the content.

All of the charities working for the welfare of people and animals who gave me permission to use quotes and offered me advice.

The BUAV for giving me permission to use their world famous cruelty free, *Leaping Bunny* logo.

About the author

Jennifer Thomson has been a vegetarian for 28 years and has always tried to live a cruelty free life. She wants to share the tips she's picked up along the way and blogs at http://greatestguidetolivingcrueltyfree.blogspot.com as well as tweeting as veggiegirl2011.

Living Cruelty Free is a one stop shop for living a more compassionate lifestyle. This is the book Jennifer wishes had been available to her all those years ago.

Jennifer is a freelance writer and the author of *Caring for Your Dog: The Essential Guide* and *Bullying – A Parent's Guide* (by Need2Know Books). She also writes fiction as Jenny Thomson.

She lives on a beautiful Scottish island with rescue dog Benjy, her partner John and hundreds of seagulls who wake her up every morning.

CONTENTS

Chapter 4   Going Vegetarian or Vegan

Chapter 5   Meat Reducers

Chapter 6   Cruelty Free Cosmetics

Useful Websites

A few words from Jennifer...

The very fact you've picked up this book means you want to live a more compassionate lifestyle; one that is kind to people and animals. This could be because you are a vegetarian or vegan and want to avoid things which involve the harming or killing of animals, whether it's for meat or cosmetics.

Or, maybe you are a meat-eater and simply want to ensure that the animals that end up on your plate had a good quality of life before they died and were allowed to roam freely and feel the sun on their faces.

Perhaps, you are simply looking to be a more ethical shopper, shunning goods made in sweatshops or using exploited child labor.

Yes, trying to live a cruelty free life means human beings are treated well too – just as Ghandi said you could judge a society by how it treats animals, we can also judge our society by how people treat their fellow human beings.

No matter how far you want to go in pursuit of a more compassionate lifestyle, the pages of this book will arm you with the facts you need to make an informed decision about the things you buy and the things you eat.

Remember, together with small steps, we can all make the world a kinder place.

How to read this book
This book can be read cover to cover and as a reference guide to dip into again and again.

If you have any questions, please feel free to contact me through my blog at
http://greatestguidetolivingcrueltyfree.blogspot.com

Jennifer

"The human spirit is not dead. It lives on in secret.... It has come to believe that compassion, in which all ethics must take root, can only attain its full breadth and depth if it embraces all living creatures and does not limit itself to mankind."

Albert Schweitzer, Nobel Peace winner in 1952, medical missionary, humanitarian and nuclear disarmament advocate.

Chapter 1
What is cruelty free?

What is cruelty free?
We all think we know what it means, but sometimes it can be difficult to define.

For the purposes of this book, living cruelty free is defined as causing no harm to animals or humans.

This can mean a number of things –
*Not buying food that was produced by killing animals.

*Not buying products that are made from the labor of workers who are not adequately paid for the work they do or treated fairly. This can mean they live in squalid, unsanitary conditions (such as having no to fresh water) and aren't paid a fair wage for the work they do.

*Not buying cosmetics that are tested on animals. Many of these tests are completely unnecessary and have been done countless times before, so they already know what the results will be.

*Not buying things that were made using obvious animal cruelty. This can mean not buying things like pillows and bedding (that contain duck feathers or down, which is often obtained by the plucking of animals whilst they are still alive, without anesthetic), and fur.

*Not buying clothing made from child slave labor. Firms have been found using child labor to make everything from dresses to footballs. Generally, these children never go to school.

Note – The key thing about being cruelty free is that you can go as far as you want. Every little helps.

Why do people decide to shop cruelty free?
You may be a vegetarian or vegan and want to avoid all products that are byproducts of the slaughterhouse, such as gelatin (also spelt gelatine) in candies (sweets) and lambskin, and products that are tested on animals.

Even if you're not a vegetarian or a meat reducer, without even realizing it, you may have already have taken steps to become a cruelty free shopper. Perhaps, you have a conscientious objection to buying certain products. Say you love horses and avoid anything that contains horsehair or anything that is made with deerskin because you think of Bambi. Or. Maybe you don't eat certain things because of the cruelty involved or because they remind you of the animal it came from.

Whatever the reason, there is a rise in the number of consumers who care how products are made and how they are sourced. That's why products carry labels saying they are cruelty free or ethically sourced, or made by workers who are paid a fair wage. If these guarantees weren't demanded by the public they wouldn't be there as businesses simply want to make as much money as possible. They may herald their ethical policies, but in most cases, they don't want to change the world. They just want to cash in on new trends in consumer behavior.

"Everyone thinks of changing the world, but no one thinks of changing himself."
Tolstoy

Why should I become a cruelty free shopper?

*Because you want to know the things you buy didn't involve cruelty towards people or animals.

*You want to know that you are doing your bit to help make the world a place where human beings and animals are shown compassion and understanding.

*The more people who buy cruelty free products, the more common cruelty free products will become. For instance, the public's anger about the testing of cosmetics on animals in the 1980's led to a number of companies shunning animal testing in favor of more reliable methods of testing products, like doing skin tests on the humans who would actually be using them. This made products that were not tested on animals more readily available. What the customer demands, the customer gets.

*If shoppers shunned cruel products then those products would no longer exist. If companies found that cruelty free products were what made them the most profit then that is what they would sell.

*You want to leave a kinder world for your children.

*To make a difference.

Can I really make a difference?
Hearing about all the bad things that happen in the world can leave us in a state of despair. How can we, as individuals, stop all the bad things from happening: put an end to all the cruelty and misery people and animals suffer from every single day?

The answer is that we can't. What we can do is change how we behave and live a more compassionate life and where we see things we don't approve of speak up. If everybody did that, together we could all change the world.

Here are some examples of people power that did make a difference –
1. It was South Africa being shunned by the international community via sanctions that led to the end of apartheid, the system whereby the majority of the population who were black were discriminated against by the government. No military action was proposed or needed.

2. In 2002, after public outrage, the USA banned the importing, exporting, sale and production of cat and dog fur. This came about after stores unknowingly sold cat and dog fur in jackets.
Note – the fur ban only applies to cat and dog fur and not any other type.

3. Fur farming is now banned in the UK. This followed successful campaigning by animal welfare campaigners and came at a time when 76 percent of people in the UK opposed the trade. Sadly, the sale of fur isn't banned.

4. In response to a 2003 campaign by *Animal Aid*, *Focus* (a UK DIY store chain) announced it would no longer sell live animals liker fish in its stores.

5. **Fairtrade** (known as **Fairtrade certified** in the USA and Canada) ensures that workers are treated and paid fairly and is one of the fastest growing brands in the world. This has come about because of the desire of millions of people to buy products that don't involve slave labor or workers living in appalling conditions.

6. There was public outrage when a TV documentary showed children making clothes in Indian refugee camps. Hundreds of people protested outside *Primark's* Oxford Street store and it was all over the media. As a result, the store sacked three of its suppliers.

7. In 2005, Inditex, who owned fashion chain *Zara*, agreed to withdraw fur from all of its 2,054 of its stores in 52 different countries. This followed a campaign by *the Coalition to Abolish the Fur Trade* (CAFT).

8. In 2011, pop star Morrissey agreed to play at Belgian musical festival Lokerse Feesten if they banned meat from their stalls. They agreed and out went the horsemeat (horsemeat is a delicacy in Belgian) and in came tofu and hummus.

9. In 2011, designer label *Versace* banned the sandblasting technique for "killer" jeans after pressure from activists. Sandblasting involves firing tiny particles of silica at the fabric to create a worn and faded look. If inhaled, Silica can cause silicosis, a pulmonary disease that can make workers ill and even kill them. Many other leading brands such as Benetton, *Levi Strauss*, *Pepe* and *Burberry*, had already banned sandblasted jeans. *The Clean Clothes Campaign* (CCC) had called for the technique to be banned. Read more about CCC and their work at www.cleanclothes.org

"No one in the world needs a mink coat but a mink."
Murray Banks

What do I need to do to become a cruelty free shopper?
The most important thing shoppers need is information. Without being informed how can we possibly know which things involve cruelty?

For instance, nobody knew that items of clothing were being made with dog and cat fur from so-called factories in China, until it was revealed in the media. Prior to that most people assumed the "fur" trim on coats was fake fur and not the real thing and some real fur was even labeled "faux fur."

Do you need to be vegetarian or vegan to be cruelty free?

Ideally not eating meat or consuming any byproducts from the meat industry is a more compassionate way to live, but you can still live a kinder life without being vegetarian or vegan. Say by choosing not to eat lobster (lobsters are thrown alive into boiling water and there is scientific evidence that they do feel pain) and Foie gras (produced by force-feeding geese and ducks until their livers expand to many times their natural size – see **Chapter 2 - Things that can never be cruelty free**).

How far do I need to go to be cruelty free?
How far you want to go is completely up to you. Small changes like not going to circuses with live animals and adopting a dog instead of buying a puppy can make a real difference (See **Chapter 9, 20 Great Ways to be Cruelty Free).** So too can having your dog neutered so that you're not adding to the problem of there being too many dogs and not enough homes.

FACT
There is no way that we can all be completely cruelty free as labeling isn't one hundred percent reliable. That is impossible. What people can be is more aware of how products are made.

How to spot Cruelty Free products
Cruelty free shoppers are avid readers of labels and packing. They look for things on labels like:

Words and phrases like these are often used -

Fairtrade (also Fair Trade)

Ethically sourced

Cruelty free – there is a Leaping Bunny logo on products to show that neither they nor their ingredients were tested on animals.

Not tested on animals – this doesn't guarantee the ingredients weren't tested on animals either by the company selling the product or their suppliers.

Recycled/recyclable

Environmentally friendly

Vegetarian/vegan

Free-range – this means something different depending on what country you're in.

Made from sustainable materials

Organic (this is kinder to the environment, humans and animals)

FACT
Just because a label says vegetarian or vegan, doesn't mean it's not tested on animals. Just that it doesn't contain animal byproducts like bone and skin and in the case of vegans honey or dairy.

"Love and compassion are necessities, not luxuries. Without them humanity cannot survive."
Dalai Lama

Are cruelty free products safe if they're not tested on animals?

Chemists know exactly what ingredients will interact safely with one another and cause allergic reactions in humans. They would never risk selling unsafe products because they would end up being sued.

And, just because products and ingredients aren't tested on animals doesn't mean they aren't tested at all. Non-animal methods are used, like skin patch testing on human volunteers or on human skin and cell cultures made in a test tube. Computer generated models are also used.

I can't afford to go cruelty free
Just because products are cruelty free does not necessary mean they will be more expensive. In fact, in many cases such as with cosmetics, the products produced without animal testing are often cheaper than ones that are tested on animals. This is because it costs vast sums of money to test on animals. You need laboratories, researchers and special equipment.

Some discount stores or supermarkets' own brand cosmetics and products will be cruelty free such as Superdrug in the UK, or they may sell cheap brands that are cruelty free. If you can't get cruelty free cosmetics in store there are dozens of online stores you can buy from. Their products are often cheaper than they would be in regular stores. You can also buy from eBay where products are often sold at a discount, especially when they are the last in a line of stock.

In the case of food, things that involve animal cruelty like veal and Foie gras are very expensive to buy.

Will people think I'm strange?
These days it's not unusual for people to be more interested in what they buy and where it comes from. You will not be alone in wanting to be a more compassionate shopper. Here are some facts:

It used to be the case that cruelty free cosmetics were hard to find, but because of consumer demand, that's no longer the case. Have a look in your local drugstore or mall and you will see that not being tested on animals is seen as a good sales tool.

Major US food companies like *Kellogg* (they bought vegetarian food label *Worthington Foods* & have the *Morningstar Farms* brand, which is meatless), Kraft Foods (they have vegetarian Boca Foods) and *Dean Foods* (they bought soy/Soya milk company *White Wave*) have either created their own line of meat substitutes or have bought companies that produce vegetarian foods. This is to cope with the demand as Americans move towards a more meatless diet.

In 2010, despite the economic downturn, spending on green products and services went up by 18 percent in the UK. Fairtrade food sales rose from 64 percent.
Source - The Co-operative Bank's annual Ethical Consumerism Report.

In the UK, frozen meat substitute sales accounted for 73 percent of vegetarian food sales between 2001 and 2003. Source - market research firm Mintel.

But, if anyone does think it's strange that you care about the origins of the things you buy, ask yourself this: how can showing compassion for other human beings and animals be considered strange?

Isn't it our compassion for other living things that defines our humanity?

Shouldn't it be not showing compassion that's considered strange?

"If a group of beings from another planet were to land on Earth... beings who considered themselves as superior to you as you feel yourself to be to other animals... would you concede them the rights over you that you assume over other animals?"
George Bernard Shaw, playwright, Nobel Prize 1925.

Chapter 2
Things that can never be cruelty free

There are certain things that under no circumstances can be described as cruelty free.

Botox
The increased popularity of Botox (Botulinium) injections has led to a sharp increase in the number of **LD50** (LD stands for lethal dose) tests being carried out on mice. In these tests, mice are injected with Botox, which is a toxin that causes paralysis and eventually death by suffocation.

For each batch, a hundred mice are poisoned and observed for days. The test is carried out to see how much of the toxin it takes to kill half of the mice. Hence LD50 – a lethal dose that kills 50 percent of test subjects. This is supposed to help determine a safe dose for human use, but mice are not humans and the reliability of these tests has been called into question.

There are non-animal tests that are considered to be more reliable, but until they come into widespread usage, Botox is not cruelty free. This is because when licenses are given for Botox toxicity testing, NO distinction is made between batches intended for the cosmetic and pharmaceutical sector (Botox does have medical uses). This way, even when it's used for cosmetic (non-medical reasons) companies manage to completely bypass the ban on testing cosmetics on animals.

FACT
If humans were given Botox intravenously (by drip straight into their bloodstream) it would kill them.

FACT
Following a legal challenge from *the BUAV* (the British Union for the Abolition of Vivisection) in 1999, the UK government announced that LD50 tests would no longer be licensed except on "exceptional scientific grounds." It is for you as an individual to decide whether having a wrinkle free forehead is worth the animal suffering.

FACT
Zyderm and *Zyplast* (often referred to as collagen, collagen implants and fillers) are the most commonly used products for smoothing wrinkles, scars and lines, especially around the lip area, but they are being replaced by newer products in the UK and USA that are also tested on animals.

Note - Zyderm and Ryplast are made from cow skins, so are not suitable for vegetarians or vegans. The similar product, *Restylane*, which was the number one filler used in America in 2011, contains no animal ingredients. However, it will probably have been tested on animals unless you are given proof to suggest otherwise.

FACT

Unless they state otherwise, most anti-wrinkle creams are probably tested on animals.

FACT

In 2011, US-based *Allergan* announced that the US *Food and Drug Administration* (FDA) had approved their way of safely testing Botox without using animal testing. Instead they would use a non-animal cell test. The company will be able to reduce animal testing by an estimated 95 percent over three years, but will still have to use animal testing for the other 5 percent. In America, testing Botox on animals is compulsory.

Chinese Medicine containing animal parts

Medicines will often contain bones from endangered animals like tigers (their powdered bone is used in many different concoctions) and from domestic animals, like dogs, cows and goats. Products may also contain rhino, leopard, shark and bear (bear farming was introduced in 1984 - bears are put in tiny cages and their bile is extracted through catheters, which is very painful). These animals are farmed so they can be killed and used in Chinese medicines.

Note – Not all Chinese medicines contain animal parts, some are based on plants. If you visit a practioner and want to know what's in their medicine, always ask. You have a right to know what you are putting in your body.

FACT
In 1993, China banned the trade in tiger bones. This was because the species was heading for extinction unless something was done. In 2007, under pressure from tiger farm owners the government lifted part of the trade ban on parts from farmed tigers. The lifting of the ban was opposed by tiger conservation groups around the world, as well as many of China's neighbors.

FACT
Shark cartilage is touted as a cancer cure in Chinese medicine, but there is no proof that is the case. It's also said to alleviate arthritis, but again there is no proof that is the case. Shark cartilage is cruelly harvested in a way that many people would consider barbaric. The fins are cut off live sharks in a method called finning, which means sharks have their fins cut off – this is the equivalent to cutting off a human being's arms and legs. Bleeding and in agony, the sharks are then tossed back into the ocean where they sink and helpless, they drown and are eaten by predators.

TIP
Some beauty remedies such as creams may contain shark cartilage, as do some alternative medicines and vitamin supplements.

FACT
The practice of finning is banned in the USA, but the sale of sharks' fins is not. In 2010, Hawaii banned people from possessing, selling, trading and distributing shark fins.

Crab

Like lobsters (see further down) crabs die painful deaths, usually by being thrown into scalding water and boiled alive, if they are not electrocuted, micro-waved or chopped up whilst still alive. That's if they survive being caught by fishermen.

Many crabs die in fishermen's nets by having their claws torn off, or through injuries they get from other crabs who in such a confined space will panic and fight with them.

FACT

During the cooking process, crabs will battle to escape, breaking off their claws as they do and causing more injuries.

Down (sometimes called feather down, duck down or goose down)

It may be well known that fur production is cruel (for more details, go down to "Fur"), but what many people don't know is that goose and duck down involves animal cruelty.

Down, the soft feathers closest to a bird's body, is used in blankets, coats, jackets, comforters, quilts, pillows and even upholstered furniture. It's well known for its warm quality. Well, it is there to keep birds warm especially in winter.

There are two ways these feathers are obtained. Firstly, the birds may have already been killed for meat production and are then plucked, but the most painful way is by plucking their feathers whilst they are still alive. This is called 'live plucking.'

There is no way to tell what method has been used, unless the product proudly boasts of the animal still being alive when it was de-feathered, which rarely happens.

This practice was first brought to the public's attention by a Swedish documentary in 2009. Showing a Hungarian goose farm where the practice was used, audiences were shocked by the sight of birds having their feathers ripped off. Many ended up paralyzed and some were left with gaping wounds that were then cruelly sewn up by workers who didn't use any pain medication on the birds.

In China, Poland and Hungary the practice of live plucking goes on all the time as the quality of the down is thought to be better when taken from live birds. Many of these birds are then used for Foie gras production (for more information on that, go down to Foie Gras).

In America, live plucking is not an industry method, but the US does import from countries that use this practice.

FACT
It's estimated that as much as 50-80% of down on sale comes from birds, who have had the feathers ripped from their bodies whilst they are still alive.

FACT
There are alternatives to down. Things like Thinsulate (commonly used in hats and other outerwear), Thermolite and Primaloft. All are synthetic and that means cruelty free.

"It is the greatest of all mistakes to do nothing because you can only do little - do what you can."
Sydney Smith, clergyman (1771- 1845)

Foie gras (pronounced fwah grah)
Of all foods this is possibly the cruelest –

1. This well-known French delicacy, translates as 'fatty liver' because that's exactly what it is. It's also called Strasbourg Pie due to the European city being a major producer of this very controversial food.

2. Foie gras is produced by force-feeding ducks or geese. This is done by workers who shove metal pipes down the birds' throats containing grain or fat. This is carried out as many as three times a day until the birds' livers bloat. Their livers can end up as much as ten times their normal size.

3. The birds are kept in cramped, tiny cages or in sheds. They have difficulty standing because of their enlarged livers and often peck their own feathers out through stress or start to eat other birds. They are also in constant pain.
PETA, *the Humane Society of the United States, the Animal Defense League*, the *RSPCA*, and the *ASPCA* have all made very vocal objections to Foie de gras.

4. According to *PETA*, an investigation they carried out at Hudson Valley Foie Gras in New York (then called Commonwealth Enterprises), found that so many ducks died when their organs ruptured from overfeeding that workers who killed fewer than 50 birds per month were given a bonus.

FACT
In 2004, California passed a law banning the sale and production of Foie gras. The ban begins in 2012. In Chicago, the force-feeding and sale of Foie de gras was banned between 2006 and 2008, but then the ban was overturned.

FACT

The force-feeding of birds has been banned in the UK, Israel, Turkey, Argentina, Austria, Germany, the Czech Republic, Finland, Italy, Luxembourg, the Netherlands, Norway, Poland, South Africa, Sweden, Switzerland, Denmark, and Israel. However, the sale of this delicacy has not. Despite the UK ban, the country is one of the biggest consumers of the product.

TIP

Foie gras may also be labeled as duck or goose pate.

FACT

Foie gras is still made in France (where they consider it part of their gastronomical heritage), Bulgaria, Spain and Canada (who are one of the major producers).

More ethical Foie gras?

There is what has been referred to as "a more ethical Foie gras." This new version is said to avoid what is termed la gavage (the force-feeding of birds by using a metal tube) - by allowing geese to stock up on extra food naturally in preparation for their normal winter migration to Africa. Once they are fat enough, they are killed.

The main problem with this method is that it costs more to produce as it takes much longer and the quality is not considered to be as good by food experts because the birds' livers never get as large as they do when they are force-fed. The demand for this type of Foie gras is low, as restaurants are charged more for what they deem to be a less quality product. Foie gras can only be produced in this way once a year as the birds are fattening up because they think they will be migrating.

FACT

In 2009, in the UK, former James Bond star, Sir Roger Moore both paid and fronted an ad in conjunction with PETA to get department store Selfridges to stop selling Foie gras. There had been plans to show undercover footage of a goose being force-fed, but that was deemed too offensive.

"As Foie gras production is too violent to show on an ad, surely this 'torture in a tin' is too violently produced for Selfridges to sell."
Sir Roger Moore, 2009, quoted in the Daily Telegraph (UK).

FACT

In 2010, vegetarian singer Leona Lewis managed to get Foie gras taken off the menu at The Brit Awards (UK music awards) by vowing not to turn up if it was available. "Foie gras is produced in such a cruel and disgusting way it would have been beyond disappointing for the record industry to endorse such a thing," explained Lewis.

Fur

Most people are in no doubt that fur is cruel. Maybe that's why in recent years the fur industry has experienced something of a worldwide decline although to fashion designers like John Paul Gaultier (in 2008 during Paris Fashion Week, he paraded models down the catwalk who were wearing real fox heads, as well as clothes made out of fur), continue to design garments using fur.

FACT

Stella McCartney, Calvin Klein and Benjamin Cho, all refuse to use fur in their designs. They are not alone and it's become trendy to go fur free.

Many different animals are killed for their fur. This includes –
foxes, rabbits, beavers, Chinchillas, minks, seals, raccoons,
bears and you may be horrified to know this, dogs and cats.

FACT
In the case of bears, hundreds of these animals are killed in
Canada for the British *Ministry of Defence* who use their fur for
the famous bearskin hats the Queen's Royal Guards wear. An
entire bearskin is needed to make just one hat. The Ministry of
Defence claim to have looked at "ethical alternatives." Animal
rights groups claim they didn't look hard enough.

The UK isn't alone in using bearskins in military hats. Many
other army regiments, usually with ceremonial duties, also
wear bearskins.

FACT
Singer Joss Stone appeared in a PETA advert in 2011, targeting
the British *Ministry of Defence*. In the ad, she was holding a
teddy bear that covered her naked body and had the slogan
"Bear Hugs, Not Bear Caps" written on it.

FACT
The UK banned fur farming in 2000. Prior to the ban, there
were eleven fur farms in the country.

TIP
Makeup brushes and applicators may be made out of animal
hair or fur. The most commonly used are horse and squirrel
hair (both animals are killed) and mink, badger and sable fur.
Mink and sable brushes are cruel byproducts of the fur
industry.

Companies like *Aveda* use synthetic brushes. Not only are they
kinder to animals, they are also kinder to your face as animal
brushes are known to cause skin irritation.

The more expensive the makeup you buy, the more likely that the brush supplied with the product is made of fur or animal hair. Not very good if you suffer from an allergy to animal hair, or fur. And it won't usually be labeled as fur.

How do animals die for fur?
Animals die in a number of ways. The bulk of them in fur farms.

FACT
There are no federal humane slaughter laws protecting animals on fur factory farms in America.

Killing methods include –

1. Being caught in steel traps. These animals can suffer in them for days before they are killed and skinned.

2. Animals on fur farms are packed into cramped cages and given meat considered unfit for human consumption. When they get their winter coats, they are killed by electrocution (by having an electrode placed in their bottoms – to make sure the coat is not damaged.) Often this doesn't work first time.

3. Factory farmed animals can also be gassed to death, have their necks broken or be injected with poison. Many are alive when they are skinned.

The Canadians slaughter seals, including baby seals, by shooting or clubbing them to death. Often hakapicks are used. They are clubs with metal hooks on the end. Dying seals are dragged along.

FACT
America banned the sale of seal fur in 1972.

FACT
In 2009, the EU voted to end the sale of all seal products.

The Chinese fur industry
According to PETA, more than half of the fur imported into America comes from China where fur production is largely unregulated. Animal welfare does not feature. Farmers are allowed to kill animals and treat them in any way that they want.

In 2009, an undercover investigation carried out by Swiss Animal Protection/EAST International found that animal cruelty was the norm on fur farms. Farmers kept animals in wired cages usually where they were exposed to the elements and animals were beaten and mistreated. Some mothers were so distressed, they killed their own babies.

When the animals are killed for their pelts, it's done by hand and they can be swung and hit against the ground. Often they don't die and merely stunned and are then skinned alive.

Cats and dogs are used in the Chinese fur trade. Although cat and dog fur is banned in America, it still manages to get into the country.

FACT
People in the UK were shocked to discover that fake garments they were buying that made no mention of fur such as jackets, boots and gloves contained the fur of cats and dogs. Thanks to a high profile campaign backed by Paul McCartney and then wife Heather Mills (25,000 signatures were collected in just one online petition), cat and dog fur imports were banned in *the EU* in 2008.

FACT
The EU (*the European Union* includes the UK, Ireland and France) fur ban was thanks to the tireless work of Member of the European parliament Struan Stevenson, who discovered the booming trade in cat and dog fur. An estimated one million of these animals were slaughtered in China alone to justify the demand for fur. In 2009, the ban came in and covered all 27 countries in the EU.

"Slaughter of these animals is horrific, with cats strangled outside their cages as other cats look on. Dogs noosed with metal wires are slashed across the groin until they bleed to death as the wire noose cuts into their throat."
European politician Struan Stevenson, speaking after the ban on cat and dog fur in the EU.

FACT
The biggest importer of Chinese fur from cats and dogs is now Russia.

How do you know where fur is produced?
You don't. Items with fur may be labeled as coming from one country, but this may not be the country where the animal it came from was farmed. Most fur now comes from China because labor costs are so low, so companies make a larger profit.

You also may not know what animal the fur comes from. Whether it's from a fox, a dog, a cat or a rabbit.

FACT
There have been many cases where real fur has been passed
off and sold as faux fur. In 2010, *The Humane Society of the
United States* conducted lab testing and found that a Phillip
Lim brand parka sold online through *Barneys* New York as
"faux fur" was in fact real animal fur. The same *Phillip Lim*
parka was sold in the Manhattan flagship store without the
"real fur" label required by New York state law.

Source – *The Fur Free Alliance*. The FFA are an international
coalition of over 35 animal protection organizations working
to bring an end to the exploitation and killing of animals for
their fur. For further information, visit:
www.infurmation.com
Please be warned, there may be disturbing images on the
website.

How do I know its faux fur and not real?
In California in 2010, a law was passed making the labeling of
fur garments compulsory in that state. The same law existed
in six other states, including New York, Delaware and New
Jersey.

Under federal law in America, most fur garments must be
labeled, but there is a loophole when it comes to items like
coats that have fur trims.

It was this loophole that led to *The Truth in Fur Labeling Act* of
2010, which came into affect on March 18th, 2011. *The Humane
Society* in the United States heralded the move because now all
fur sold in the US, regardless of price must be labeled as fur.
Prior to this, fur garments under the price of $150 did not have
to be labeled as fur.

Note – Under the new law, fur items brought in by retailers before March 18th, 2011 did NOT have to be labeled as real fur, although it was suggested that shops voluntarily label them as fur.

"With more than one million items of clothing or accessories being sold with animal fur in the U.S. each year, it only makes sense that consumers know what kind of fur they are wearing.
There is an assumption out there that if a garment isn't labeled it must be fake this isn't always the case. People have a right to know if they are buying dog fur or a polyester blend. It shouldn't be a mystery."
California Assemblywoman, Fiona Ma

Is it real fur?
The problem of real fur being labeled as fake fur is so bad that animal charities have advised people on how to tell the difference. They stress that you can't tell just by look or touch. Fur can be dyed and shaved to change its appearance and feel. As a result of the demise of the market for fur, there are companies trying to pass real fur off as fake.

The best test apparently is the burn test (not very helpful if you want to check it out before you buy). However, this test can tell you whether you've been misled into buying real fur. To do this, cut or pull out some hairs from the garment. Carefully light the hairs with a lighter or a match. If it smells like your hair when it's caught in a hairdryer, it's fur.

Another test that is meant to be reliable, involves a pin. With faux fur, the pin will go right through the base of the garment. With real fur it won't.

The Coalition to Abolish the Fur Trade offer advice on their website at www.caft.org.uk

Please be warned, there may be disturbing images.

FACT
In the UK, Harrods is the only department store that still sells fur although the production of fur is illegal in the country.

FACT
It's not just clothing that can use real fur. Soft toys may also be made out of fur. Usually this is from factory-farmed rabbits. In the UK, sleeping cats that looked like the real thing were sold to unwitting customers who had no idea real fur was used. Cat and dog fur has also been found on similar toys and ornaments.

Lobster
Considering that many lobsters are lobbed into boiling pans whilst they are still alive whilst the others are killed by people wielding knives and slitting them from head to tail, it's not difficult to see how eating them is considered cruel. Those who defend the practice of boiling claim that the crustaceans don't have a central nervous system and that means they can feel no pain. If you watch a lobster in a boiling pan you will see it throwing its body around, trying to escape.

In the journal *Science*, researcher Gordon Gunter described this method of killing lobsters as "unnecessary torture."

Whilst lobsters are in tanks waiting to be bought, the people selling them won't feed them. This is to stop the tank filling with ammonia from lobster excrement, as too much can kill lobsters and cooks want them to be fresh. Because they are not fed, these creatures can starve to death, or in desperation, try to eat each other.

FACT

Lobsters carry their young for nine-months like humans do and can also live to one hundred. Scientists have also determined that they can feel pain.

FACT
Lobsters are caught and taken away from their natural habitat then stored in freezing conditions in a semi-conscious state before they are killed. When they are boiled alive it can take up to seven minutes for them to die.

"Why are we appalled by the cruelty companion animals suffer, yet we ignore the suffering of lab animals? Do they not deserve the same protections?"
Anon

Medicines
Unfortunately, in most cases laws insist that all medicines must be tested on animals before they are used on humans in order for companies to be given licenses to sell them. Scientists argue that this is necessary to make sure the medicines are safe, but the truth is that it's only through testing on humans that you can tell how safe these medicines are to humans. No animal is genetically the same as a human being.

There are many cases where medicines that were tested on animals and appeared to be safe have turned out to be very dangerous to humans. Take Thalidomide for instance. Developed as an anti-sickness drug for pregnant women, Thalidomide had disaster consequences for many of the people who took it.

Babies were born with deformities, many with missing limbs as Thalidomide damaged the fetuses in the womb. Other women tragically miscarried. As a result of these tragedies, the drug was banned in the 1960's. Yet animal tests didn't have the same results.

FACT
There are testing methods that do NOT involve using animals that are more reliable then animal testing that will, hopefully, one day, replace all animal testing, including human skin cells created in a test tube. Some of these methods range from creating human cells including skin in a test tube, to testing on humans themselves, are considered much more reliable than animal testing. We may soon see a day, when we may no longer need to test any drugs on animals.

FACT
When it comes to prescription drugs, Beagles are one of the most experimented on animals. Drugs for cancer, heart disease, heart attacks and infectious diseases are tested on Beagles who are used because of their gentle, friendly nature and desire to please. Some of the tests conducted on them are considered barbaric by many.

One test involves them being forced to inhale chemicals by having a gas mask type device forcibly latched onto their noses and faces. They also have substances dripped into their eyes, have tubes inserted into their stomachs to force-feed them and are restrained whilst they have substances pumped directly into their bloodstreams.

In most cases anesthetic is not used and these dogs suffer in agony.

In many cases, these tests have been done countless times before in other countries.

FACT

If you're vegetarian or vegan and want to avoid gelatin (gelatine) in medicines, you can buy veggie capsules or veggie tabs instead. You can buy them empty and put the medicine in them yourself. Other medicines like Prozac can also come in liquid form. If you're prescribed a medication by your doctor, always ask if there is a non-gelatin alternative. Often there is.

FACT

One of the reason animal tests are not reliable, is that diseases are artificially induced. A disease that is generated is not the same as a disease that someone has developed often over time through their environment or diet.

TIP

If you want to end the testing of medicines on animals, then back the charities that are looking to replace animal experiments. This includes organizations like *the British Union for the Abolition of Vivisection (The BUAV)* who are leading the way.

For more details, visit the following organization's websites - www.buav.org and click on "**Humane science**."
The National Anti-Vivisection Society at www.navs.org.uk

Animal Defenders International is a global organization who also campaign to replace animal experiments www.ad-international.org

The Dr Hadwen Trust for Humane Research (DHT) offers grants to scientists in the UK to carry out non-animal experiments www.drhadwentrust.org

TIP

Give money to charities that commission non-animal research for conditions like cancer and Alzheimer's. Experts say that the many years and millions that have been spent using animals to find cures by conducting experiments are wasteful and have not advanced medical science.

To read more about charities that don't fund animal testing on their behalf and those that do, go to www.peta.org/issues/animals-used-for-experimentation/charities.aspx

The Physicians Committee for Responsible Medicine (PCRM) has a searchable database of charities that don't fund animal research at www.humaneseal.org/search.cfm
You can search for charities in the USA, Canada, the UK and Australia. Charities awarded their Humane Charity Seal of Approval are those that are committed to advancing medical research without using animals.

In the UK, Animal Aid has a list of charities that only commission non-animal medical research and those that do www.animalaid.org.uk/h/n/CAMPAIGNS/experiments/ALL/281
Note – the list is constantly updated and the policies of some charities may change.

FACT

Despite the many millions poured into animal research, an effective animal model (one that is truly representative of a human being) hasn't yet been identified. This is no surprise as HIV stands for Human Immunodeficiency Virus. This means HIV is specifically a human virus. Animals can't contract it.

"What good does it do you to test something (a vaccine) in a monkey? You find five or six years from now that it works in the monkey, and then you test it in humans and you realize that humans behave totally differently from monkeys, so you've wasted five years."
Dr. Mark Feinberg, a leading AIDS researcher.

Mega dairies
One thing that could also have been added to this list of things that can never be cruelty free, is milk produced by cows in mega dairies. These cows are kept inside in crowded and dimly lit sheds or warehouses, for the majority of their lives and these dairies have a "zero grazing" system (the cows are never put out to pastures in fields). This has been linked to health problems in the cows that people fear could be passed onto humans through the cows' milk.

Cows in mega dairies have a greater chance of infection caused by living in such closed, crowded quarters and never being out in the fresh air.

These types of farms are common in America and there is a move to have them throughout Europe.

FACT
In 2011, a campaign led by animal rights organizations and Compassion in World Farming (set up by a dairy farmer Peter Roberts in 1967), managed to get a plan by Nocton Dairies withdrawn. Nocton wanted to build what would have been the first mega dairy in Western Europe in Lincolnshire in the UK. It would have housed almost 4,000 cows. Over 72,000 people signed a petition opposing the plan, including local residents.

It's up to you to decide whether you think drinking milk produced by mega dairies is supporting a cruel trade or not.

•

FACT

No milk is produced without cruelty. Mothers have their young taken away so the milk they produce for their children can be used by humans. Often the male baby calves are killed to be eaten or put in veal crates. The mothers are often pumped full of steroids so that they will produce more milk that nature intended to meet the huge demand for milk in the West.

FACT

Milk has been linked with breast cancer. In China where they don't consume milk products, their rate of breast cancer amongst women is a fraction of what it is in the West where dairy is part of people's everyday diets. According to Cancer Research UK, the risk of a woman getting breast cancer in her life is one in eight. In the USA the rate is similar.

TIP

Try soy (Soya) milk or rice or oat milk. They are much better for you and can help reduce cholesterol. You can also get nut-based milks.

Sheepskin

Unlike wool, in the case of sheepskin, the sheep does have to be killed first–

As its name suggests, sheepskin, is more than just wool. In fact it's the equivalent of wearing fur because the wool is still attached to the skin when it's taken off. Hence the word sheepskin.

Ugg boots are made from sheepskin and so are many pieces of footwear like slippers, as well as other things like coats and jackets. It will say sheepskin on the label, as it's in a shop's best interests to state this as it makes the item worth more.

Faux sheepskin can be just as warm as the real thing and is readily available at a much lower cost that real sheepskin – to your pocket as well as to the sheep.

You have to decide whether to wear sheepskin or not, but there's a strong argument for saying it's the equivalent to wearing fur because you are wearing an animal's skin. The main argument for wearing sheepskin is the same one for wearing leather - that the animal was dead anyway, because sheepskin comes from lambs and sheep killed to be eaten. The makers of *Uggs* say that no animal cruelty is involved because sheepskin is a natural byproduct of the food industry.

The main argument against, is that an animal was killed for the sheepskin; therefore its production was far from cruelty free.

TIP

You can buy boots that look like Ugg boots at a fraction of the cost, which don't contain sheepskin. These days, synthetic fabrics are of a good quality. Usually they are labeled as containing sheepskin (as it justifies the high cost of the finished product), but not always.

TIP

Sheepskin can also sneak its way into furniture like sofas, chairs, cushions as well as bedding, handbags and children's clothing. And, believe it or not, shampoo.

These things will usually cost a lot more than their non-sheepskin containing products, but they might not always be labeled. If they are labeled, they will say something like "Pure sheepskin" and "real sheepskin."

FACT

Pamela Anderson blamed herself for starting the craze for Ugg boots when she was on Baywatch because she used to wear them with her famous red swimsuit.

> *"I used to wear them with my red swimsuit to keep warm -*
> *never realizing that they were skin! Do not buy UGGs! Buy*
> *Stella McCartney or Juicy boots."*
> Pamela Anderson

FACT

It's not just sheepskin that involves cruelty. Australia produces most of the world's merino wool. Many farmers there use a process called mulesing, which means a device that looks like garden shears is used to cut away huge chunks of skin and flesh away from merino lambs so that the animals won't get something called fly strike that can kill them. Farmers have a choice to breed fly strike resistant sheep, but choose not to do this.

Veal

Veal has a delicate taste and texture, which is why it's considered such a delicacy. Mention the word and although people may have tried it, they are probably unaware of how it is made.

Veal is basically made from the meat of male baby calves. These calves are taken away from their mothers, sometimes when they are no more than a few hours old, but usually when they are days old. They will never see their mothers again. They are placed in wooden crates so small they are unable to turn around, never mind walk and they are deprived of any light and human contact. Some calves are chained by their necks to stop them moving at all. They are fed mainly on a milk diet. This is to ensure that their meat is pale in color. Many become anemic (anemic) because of their restrictive diet and lack of sunlight.

After four to five months, they are transported to the slaughterhouse in trucks where they are killed to produce what is described as 'milk-fed veal.' By this stage, most of the calves are unable to walk.

Not all veal calves suffer this fate. Some are killed within hours or days of being born to be used as low-grade veal, which is often called bob veal.

Although not used as veal, the female calves are often taken away from their mothers too. They are put in small huts until they are old enough to have calves themselves and produce milk

FACT
When cows have their calves taken away from them, they react by bellowing and get into a distressed state just like human mothers would if they were forcibly separated from their babies.

Veal crates and the law
Since 1990, veal crates have been outlawed in the UK on animal welfare grounds. Since 2007, they have also been banned in the EU.

Veal is still produced in the UK, but there is a low demand for this meat because of the cruelty involved. In the UK, veal calves are given bedding and better food than their crated counterparts. Up to the age of eight-weeks-old, they are kept in pens where they can turn around and see other calves. When they are older, they are kept in large sheds with large groups of other calves, but in cramped conditions.

FACT
Live calves are still being shipped from the UK to other countries where they will end up in crates for veal.

FACT
The state of Colorado introduced new legislation to phase out veal crates for calves in 2008. This came as a result of negotiations between the Humane Society of the United States and agricultural groups.

FACT
Due to public pressure, The American Veal Association has announced they plan to phase out the use of crates by 2017. Veal sourced from other countries may still be crate raised.

"Choosing free-range eggs and reading food labels, to ensure you buy processed products containing free-range eggs, can make a big difference to the quality of life for hens."
Jane Howorth, Chief Executive of the British Hen Welfare Trust.

Chapter 3
Going free-range & cage-free

The attitude of consumers is changing - at least in the UK. Where once it seemed no one cared about the eggs they fried in the morning coming from battery hens, free-range sales outstripped caged hen eggs for the first time in 2008 in the UK, according to *the British Egg Information Service*.

This is because of all the publicity about battery hens and the miserable existence they endure to meet the UK's egg needs.

Most UK supermarkets also only use free-range eggs in their own brand products and some stores like *Marks & Spencer's*, *Waitrose*, *Sainsbury's* and *Morrisons* have stopped selling eggs from caged hens altogether. This is due to declining demand and the need to be seen as more ethical.

The change in shopping habits has shown that British consumers value compassion for animals over cost, as free-range eggs are more expensive than ones produced by battery hens. Free-range eggs tend to cost more money because the hens have a better quality of life and are often fed high quality grain (many hens are fed chicken meal, which is basically dead hens).

The British Hen Trust

In the UK, hens have their own charity to look out for their welfare. The British Hen Welfare Trust (formerly known as The Battery Hen Trust), not only re-homes battery hens, they also try and educate the public about hen welfare. For more details, visit their site at www.bhwt.org.uk

The charity has a number of celebrity supporters including, Chef Jamie Oliver.

In 2010, the charity celebrated finding a home for their 200th bird. Fittingly enough for a moment that required the popping of some champagne corks, the hen was called Fizz.

The situation in United States and Canada

Sadly, in the USA and Canada things are very different. The majority of eggs are from caged hens, and the criteria for eggs to be described as free-range are different to those in the UK and are nowhere near as strict. However, this could be changing in America.

In 2011, work by *Farm Sanctuary and the Humane Society of the United States* activists in California, Ohio, Washington, and Oregon has brought the United Egg Producers to the table. They agreed to aggressively support federal legislation that would lessen the suffering of 280 million laying hens.

The legislation would mean –
1. The eventual phasing out of the existing battery cages that are so small hens can't stretch out one wing never mind two.

2. The introduction of cages that would offer hens twice the space they currently have.

3. Egg producers offering what are called "environment enrichments" for hens. This could include perching posts, nesting boxes and scratching areas.

4. Making it mandatory to put labeling on the box of eggs saying exactly how they were produced. Say 'eggs from cage free hens' and 'eggs from caged hens' so that shoppers can make an informed choice.

5. Improving the standards of euthanasia (the way hens are killed, including baby chicks).

6. Cutting down on the amount of Ammonia in the hens' environment. In excessive amounts, Ammonia is dangerous to both the humans who work in henhouses and to the birds.

7. Stopping the practice of starving birds to make them molt. This is used to interfere with the laying process.

8. Restricting the sale of egg and egg products that fail to meet those standards.

Note – Although better for the hens, these improvements don't mean hens are free-range i.e. allowed out in the open.

"For too long, animals on factory farms have had no federal protection from even the most heinous abuse. This new federal bill would ensure modest yet historic improvements for egg-laying hens, and we encourage Washingtonians to urge their lawmakers to enact it as soon as possible."
Gene Baur, president and co-founder of *Farm Sanctuary*.

FACT

By January 2012, battery cages will be banned across the EU (the European Union that includes the UK, Ireland and France). The new colony cages provide a third more of the space currently legally required by each bird, along with a nest, perching space and a scratching area. Animal welfare charities claim these "enriched" cages still do not give the birds enough space and are still battery cages. Birds will never get to see the sun or indulge in natural behaviors. Hens are very sociable animals.

In America, the future is bleaker for battery hens because 95% of eggs sold come from factory farmed birds, although as previously mentioned, the conditions they are forced to live in could improve in the future, but not sufficiently for most people in animal welfare.

Battery hens - So, what's all the fuss about? Is the battery hen industry cruel?

Judge for yourself by the following facts, which refer to hens in the UK (in countries like America, the conditions hens live in are much worse) –

1. All hens are in cages, sometimes with up to four other birds. There isn't enough room for them to turn around in.

2. Legal requirements mean each given bird is given just under three quarters the size of an A4 sheet of paper in the UK.

3. The cages are usually in large sheds with one cage packed on top of another.

4. These hens are kept indoors and never see sunlight. Any light they get is artificial.

5. They all have to be de-beaked (have their beaks trimmed) to prevent them attacking each other, their selves or workers, because of the stress of confinement. De-beaking is done when the birds are as young as one day old and then again at about seven weeks old. A hot machine blade is often used and the process is painful. It's been likened to humans having their hands chopped off.

6. Many birds die because of diseases they get caused by having to sit in their own poop.

7. Once they stop laying eggs, they are killed for pet food.

8. Rescued battery hens can hardly walk, are scared of the outdoors and need to have their long nails clipped.

FACT
In Australia, it's estimated that more 95% of all hens have had their beaks trimmed and that includes on free-range farms. In Switzerland, Sweden and Austria, and hens rarely have their beaks trimmed.

FACT
In 2010, the UK government backed out of a ban on de-beaking that was to come into force in 2011. *The Farm Animal Welfare Council* (FAW) still insists they want an eventual ban on the practice. *Compassion in World Farming* (CiFW) had also backed the ban.

The Welfare of Laying Hens Directive stipulates that for eggs to be termed "free-range," hens must have continuous daytime access to runs which are mainly covered with vegetation and with a maximum stocking density of 2,500 birds per hectare.'
Source - British Egg Industry Council

In America, it's a different story...

Free-range eggs in America
In America, USDA regulations apply only to poultry (birds like hens) and indicate that animals have been allowed to go outside. The USDA regulations however do not specify the quality or size of the outside area, or the amount of time the animal must spend outside or be able to go outside. Hens can spend as little as five minutes outside and still have their eggs labeled as free-range.

In the UK, this wouldn't be allowed, but there was one case where caged eggs were passed off as free-range so the seller could make more money.

TIP
In America, free-range is often confused with 'yarding' where hens are kept fenced in yards, but this is not the same as free-range.

FACT
Most hens in America have their beaks trimmed or are de-beaked, which is the same thing.

Free-range eggs in Canada
In Canada, free-range eggs come from hens and chickens who are allowed to roam freely outside. These eggs will have the **Animal Welfare Approved Eggs** label.

Labels on eggs that are not free-range often have things like farm fresh and all natural making you think of hens running free, when they're actually in cages or sheds. Other misleading terms include cage free or free run. This means that hens may be allowed to roam freely inside the sheds where they are housed, but there isn't much room to do so and some hens end up cannibalizing (eating) their fellow kind out of frustration, boredom or hunger.

FACT
Most eggs sold in Canada are from battery hens.

FACT
Canadian free-range egg producers do not have to have their products certified unless they also claim they are organic. This means anyone can label their eggs free-range.

Eggs may even be called free-range when the hen that laid them has to go in a cage or back in a shed. Nor does the label guarantee that the bird has been fed healthy food.

Free range eggs in Australia
In Australia, 80% of eggs are from caged birds. Considering it's a country full of wide, open spaces that may come as a shock.

There is NO legal, enforceable legislation for the standards of free-range eggs in Australia. This means that it's very easy for egg producers to label their eggs free-range.

There's also a difference in standards usually this involves the amount of time they are allowed outside, whether they are given growth promoters (steroids) and whether they have their beaks trimmed or not.

TIP
If you want to ensure your eggs are truly free range, the only way to do it is to get your own laying hens.

"God loved the birds and invented trees. Man loved the birds and invented cages."
Jacques Deval

Free-range eggs in the UK
In the UK, free-range means the animals are allowed to roam freely without being contained in any manner like in a cage or a shed. This means they live most of their lives in the outdoors, but they have access to shelter.

The UK has the strongest legislation for free-range eggs in the world.

Note – eggs from free run hens in the UK, are not to be confused with free-range. Free run simply means they have free run of their environment, which in most cases is a dark shed. These hens don't usually have access to the outdoors and natural sunlight.

FACT
In 2010, *Hellmann's* announced that they would only be using cage free eggs in their products in America and Canada. This followed on from a similar pledge to do the same thing in Western Europe (including the UK) a year earlier. The eggs will be American Humane Certified, which means the hens are indoors only hens, but they are not in cages.

Is free-range the same as organic?
All organic hens are free-range hens, but most free-range hens are not organic.

There are a number of differences between free-range and organic egg systems in the UK, which explains why organic, free-range eggs are that much more expensive –

*Free-range hens are almost always de-beaked, organic hens are not.

*Organic hens are not given genetically modified food. Free-range hens can be.

*Organic hens are not given antibiotics, but free-range ones usually are.

*Organic hens are not fed with any animal by-products like dead hens, free-range hens can be.

*Free-range hens can be kept in cramped conditions, organic ones roam free.

*Organic hens are not given feed that has been treated with pesticides or that has added colorants. Organic means no chemicals are used.

Note – Don't assume all organic eggs come from free-range egg systems unless it says organic and free-range on the box. Organic usually refers to the hens being fed natural, good quality food and them not being given antibiotics and growth hormones. It doesn't always mean hens that are allowed to roam free and indulge in normal behaviors.

What are barn eggs?
Barn hens are kept in large windowless sheds. They have perches and bedding and are free to roam in the sheds, but they aren't usually allowed to go outside.

Barn hens have better lives than battery hens, but are not free-rangeland certainly not organic. Often the sheds they are in are cramped full of other birds.

What do the codes on UK eggs mean?
In the UK, eggs must be coded by law. Eggs are routinely checked using ultraviolet lights that show up the wire marks that are on battery hen eggs.

The first number refers to the farming method.
0 – organic
1 – Free-range
2 – Barn
3 – Cage

This is followed by the country of origin and the farm ID, which tells you exactly where these eggs came from.

Is there an egg coding system in America?
No, in America, there is no coding system for eggs. Phrases like free roaming and all natural, are often used. This also does not mean the eggs are free-range. The only word on labels regulated by the US government is organic.

Are free-range eggs better for me, and if so why?
Professor Michael Crawford, of the institute of brain chemistry and human nutrition at London Metropolitan University, found that free-range hens produce more nutritious eggs.

This is no surprise, as unlike their caged friends they are not left in diseased ridden cages to lie in their own mess and to peck away at the birds sharing those cages because of the stress.

Why do free-range eggs cost more?

Free-range hens and chicken eggs cost more because the animals are generally fed better than factory hens and are given more space to roman in. In the UK, they also must have access to the open air. This means egg producers need more land.

Note in America, the rules on free-range hens and chickens are much laxer. Having as little as five minutes in the outdoors is considering sufficient to describe their eggs as free-range.

In Canada, free-range means the same as it does in the UK i.e. hens that are allowed to run about outside.

Why do some people still say free-range eggs are cruel?
Egg producers have no use for male chicks (they can't lay eggs), so they're killed by crushing or gassing. Many are fed in handfuls and dropped alive into a mincing machine in a process known as IMD - **Instantaneous Mechanical Destruction**. This was shown in undercover footage by *Viva!* (*Vegetarians International Voice for Animals*) in the UK when they filmed at a hatchery.

Both of these methods are approved by the UK's Government's food and farming department, *Defra*, and the *Humane Slaughter Association*. Yet if you did that to a pet bird, you would be prosecuted.

FACT
Whether birds go into a free-range system or not they still have their beaks cut off when they are chicks.

Is there such a thing as free-range meat?

No meat is ever cruelty free. That's impossible, as killing animals can never be humane. What you can get is meat from animals that are treated in a more humane way when they were alive. This usually means free-range meat.

The benefits of free-range products extend further than animals having a better life. Eating free-range meat is also meant to be better for the health of the consumer as animals raised in a natural way are more likely to be high quality meat when they are dead.

"Who can believe that there is no soul behind those luminous eyes!"
Theophile Gautier

FACT
Most people say they are against factory farming, but 80 percent of meat comes from factory.
Source – *Viva!*

More Ethical Meat
More ethical meat means -

1. Animals are allowed to indulge in their normal behaviors. This means being allowed to be with their own kind, to be outdoors but to also have protection from the weather.

2. They're raised in a natural environment. This can mean sheep and cows being allowed to graze in open fields and not locked away in sheds, crates or cages of any kind.

3. When they are being transported to be killed, their journeys are as short as possible. This means not being confined to tiny crates, left without bedding or water and not being seen by a vet if they are in pain during the journey.

4. Unfortunately, there is no way of killing animals for food that is without cruelty.

5. What there are is more humane ways of killing them, so that death is as quick and pain free as possible to minimize their suffering. They should also not be watch on as their friends are slaughtered.

In a nutshell, free-range meat.

TIP
Organic meat does not mean the same as free range. Organic can be free range, but not always.

Organic generally means the animals have been given no antibiotics, growth hormones and fed on GMO feed. Nor have they been turned into cannibals by being forced to eat food made up of their own kind. The Mad Cow Disease epidemic in the UK was caused by farmers feeding cows who are vegetarians, a feed that contained parts of cows and sheep.

They are also more likely to be raised in a more humane way.

Free-range meat
The following types of meat can be classified as free-range if certain criteria is met -

Pork – Free-range pregnant sows should be kept in groups and are should be provided with straw for bedding, rooting and chewing. Pigs should live out in the open, but have access to shelter.

According to Animal Aid booklet, The Trouble With Farming: 'The guiding principle governing free-range farming is that animals are able to roam freely. However, some certified free-range systems allow farmers to confine pregnant sows in metal farrowing crates in which their piglets are born and suckled. And, around 90 per cent of free-range piglets are actually "finished" inside crowded, barren sheds, with slatted floors. (*Pye-Smith, C. 2003. Batteries not included, organic farming and animal welfare. Soil Association production, labeling and control.*)

Chicken & Turkey - Free-range chickens and turkeys should have continuous access to an outdoor range during the daytime. The range should be largely covered in vegetation and allow more space. Access to fresh air and daylight means better eye and respiratory health. The birds are able to exercise and exhibit natural behavior resulting in stronger, healthier legs. Free-range systems often use slower-growing breeds of chickens and turkeys.

Beef – Cows should be allowed out to pasture and are preferably not be given any hormones or steroids.

Lambs are able to roam freely in fields.

Game – This refers to all meat from animals that are hunted and not farmed for food like deer (also called venison, which comes from baby deer), rabbit and duck (America only, as in the UK no one hunts ducks). It would be wrong to assume that all game is free-range because there are deer and duck farms. Pheasants are also farmed and often the ones hunting parties shoot are birds that have been kept in cages and they are therefore no more free-range than battery hens.

FACT
Killing baby deer is banned in many American states.

TIP
Organic meat is not to be confused with free-range. Organic can mean animals are kept indoors much like battery hens.

What is the Freedom Food scheme?
It was set up by animal charity *the RSPCA* (the Royal Society for the Protection of Cruelty to Animals) who cover England and Wales in the UK, and aimed to improve the conditions that animals reared for food are kept in.

The scheme has faced criticism after *the Happy Egg Company*, who were given *Freedom Food* accreditation were investigated by *Viva!* who found the conditions the hens were kept in could hardly be described as freedom. To find out more, visit the Viva! page http://www.viva.org.uk/what-we-do/happy-egg-company

How does the scheme work?
Every company that applies for the scheme must meet minimum welfare standards, which include a Freedom Food inspector visits each producer once a year to make sure standards have been maintained.

To find out more, visit www.rspca.org.uk/freedomfood

Whilst any scheme to improve the lives of farm animals is welcomed by animal welfare charities, some accuse the scheme's standards of being too low.

"If slaughterhouses had glass walls, everyone would be a vegetarian."
Sir Paul McCartney.

Chapter 4
Going vegetarian or vegan

One of the best ways live a cruelty free life, is by going vegetarian because by doing that you're not contributing to the number of animals that are being killed for meat and products containing slaughterhouse byproducts like gelatin (gelatine).

You could go even further and go vegan to avoid all animal products like leather, wool, eggs, milk and honey.

In 2008, American magazine, *Vegetarian Times*, conducted Vegetarianism in America study, which found some interesting facts –
*7.3million Americans are vegetarian.
*22.8million live a vegetarian inclined lifestyle. This means they were actively trying to eat less meat. People who do this are often referred to as meat reducers.

In the UK, there are is an estimated 4 million people who are vegetarian. Around 5 percent of that number, are vegans who consume and use no animal products at all.

Vegetarians
There are different types of vegetarians, although most vegetarians will simply call themselves vegetarian and say whether they eat eggs and drink milk.

ALL vegetarians abstain from eating meat and that includes fish and fowl. This is usually because they disagree with killing animals for food when there is so much more cruelty free food available. Most vegetarians will not wear items that are made from killing animals and this includes leather and fur.

Lacto-Vegetarians (also called lactarians) don't eat animal flesh (meat) and that includes fish and poultry (chicken, turkey etc). They do drink milk and eat products containing milk. But they don't eat eggs. This is the most common type of vegetarian in India where the majority of the world's vegetarians live. Most vegetarians there are Hindus.

Ovo-lacto Vegetarians don't eat meat, including poultry and fish. However they do consume dairy and egg products (usually only free-range eggs). This is the most common type of vegetarian in the US, UK, Canada and Australia.

There are also the **pescetarians**, who don't eat meat but who do eat fish. They are not considered true vegetarians and are often dismissed as pseudo-vegetarians because true vegetarians do not eat animal flesh of any kind. Pescetarians tend to eat the diet they do for health reasons and not because they disagree with animals being eaten, which puts them in the minority.

FACT
Before the word vegetarian was coined around 1840, the term used was "vegetable diet." Some people referred to themselves as **Pythagoreans** after the ancient Greek Pythagoras (570c-495BC) who set up a school in Italy. Pythagoras believed in the transmigration of the soul (reincarnation) and because of that his followers were vegetarian. He also believed that men and women were equal, an unusual belief at that time.

Vegans

The word vegan was invented by founder of *The Vegan Society*, Donald Watson, in the 1940's. **World Vegan Day**, the date of the society's founding, November 1, is now celebrated every year.

"I was surrounded by interesting animals. They all 'gave' something: the farm horse pulled the plough, the lighter horse pulled the trap, the cows 'gave' milk, the hens 'gave' eggs and the cockerel was a useful 'alarm clock' – I didn't realize at that time that he had another function too. The sheep 'gave' wool. I could never understand what the pigs 'gave,' but they seemed such friendly creatures – always glad to see me." Donald Watson, inventor of the word vegan, explaining his decision to become vegan. It was realizing what the 'pigs gave' at the age of 14 that made him turn vegetarian.

Although vegans are a type of vegetarian, they are not to be confused with vegetarians as they do not eat or use any animal products at all. This includes eating anything or using products that don't involve the death of animals and cruelty, like consuming honey or wearing wool. Vegans don't use leather either.

It can be very tricky being a vegan as many products that appear vegan are not. For instance, some breakfast cereals have vitamin D added that comes from sheep's wool and the majority of condoms contain milk proteins, and are not considered vegan. There are vegan condoms that exist, which use cocoa powder. Candy (sweets) may also be glazed with beeswax, which vegans don't eat.

Why do people go vegan/vegetarian?
1. For animal welfare reasons - They don't want to eat animals. Perhaps they think the way animals are farmed and killed is wrong, or they simply think it's immoral to kill another living thing to eat when there are so many other things humans can eat instead.

2. For lifestyle beliefs - They don't think it's morally wrong to eat animals, they just think it's healthier and is less likely to make them put on weight. This type of vegetarian is in the minority.

3. For religious reasons - Some sects of Hinduism are vegetarian. Followers of the Jainism religion believe that all sentient beings are equal and don't eat animals. About half of all Buddhists are vegetarian. Some Sikhs also believe it's wrong to eat meat.

4. For health reasons - Going veggie is meant to help with a variety of conditions, including heart disease, high cholesterol, type 2 diabetes, osteoporosis, arthritis, allergies, asthma, environmental illness, hypertension, gout, gallstones, hemorrhoids, kidney stones, ulcers, colitis, premenstrual syndrome, anxiety, and depression. The list is a very long one.

FACT
India has the most vegetarians of any country in the world. An estimated 1.2billion people, but eating meat is on the increase as it becomes more affordable and better quality.

"One day I was helping my mom make dinner, cutting up a chicken, and I hit a tumor with the knife. There was pus and blood all over the place. That was enough for me." – Actor Josh Hartnett

Is it safe for children to be vegan or vegetarian?

The key is for everyone is to have a balanced diet containing foods that have all the things your body needs like protein, vitamins and minerals. This is vital whether you follow a traditional diet of eating meat and animal by products or have a diet with no animal products.

In the case of a vegetarian diet, it is perfectly safe for children to be on this diet as long as that diet is balanced. However, in the case of vegan children, they may need to take supplements like B12. This is not always the case as vegan parents tend to be more knowledgeable about nutrition than other parents and cook food from scratch, so they tend to serve up much less processed food with nasty Trans fats and e numbers that can cause obesity and hyperactivity in children.

TIP

Always seek advice before changing diet, especially a child's. If you are a woman who is vegan or vegetarian, remember that if you have any deficiencies your baby's nutritional needs will not be met through breastfeeding. You may have to take supplements if your diet is lacking in certain vitamins and minerals.

Please see **Vegetarian and Vegan Organizations** at the back of book for details of organizations where you can seek advice.

How animals are killed for food

In America

The Humane Slaughter Act (also known as *the Humane Methods of Livestock Slaughter Act*), is a federal law passed in 1958 that is supposed to protect animals during their slaughter. In reality it is a weak act.

Under the act, animals must be unconscious when they are killed. This is done by stunning. The Act does not cover fish and birds such as hens, chickens, ducks and turkeys. This is seen as surprising by animal welfare groups as Americans consume a lot of poultry.

The Act has been criticized for a number of reasons –
1. Not being enforced properly by the United States Department of Agriculture (USDA). Inspectors claim they cannot enforce the law because they continually have difficulty getting into slaughterhouses.

2. Slaughterhouses are accused of breaching the law and not being penalized for it. The Washington Post reported that in 1998, a Texas beef company cited 22 times for chopping the hooves off cattle, whilst the animals were still alive, escaped any punishment.

3. Having no power. Under the revised act of 1978, inspectors were allowed to stop the slaughter line if they saw the act being flouted. They could do little else.
Not covering all animals killed for meat. Under this law, there is no requirement for how birds should be killed.

4. Not covering the welfare of the animals in the months or years up to their deaths.
Being out of date and not reflecting modern standards of animal welfare and more compassionate practices.

FACT
Hens, chickens and ducks are placed head first on a conveyor belt whilst fully conscious, and have their necks cut by a mechanical cutter. If the cutter works, they bleed to death. If it doesn't work, they are alive when they are immersed in scalding water so their feathers come off.

FACT

Cattle are stunned with a captive bolt gun and then have their throats cut. They bleed to death, usually whilst shackled and hung upside down. Sometimes they are killed with electricity.

FACT

Animals intended for halal or kosher meat, are usually not stunned for religious reasons.

The UK

Most animals in the UK are stunned with a captive bolt pistol before they are killed because all animals must be stunned before they are slaughtered in the UK (see below for religious exemptions to the law). This is meant to make them unconscious so they feel no pain but there is no proof this is the case and sometimes the stunning doesn't work, and either has to be done again or no one notices because animals are killed in an assembly line.

Once stunned, animals are shackled by a hind leg and hoisted above the ground. A slaughter man then cuts the animal's throat, using a very sharp knife. This severs the major blood vessels in the animals neck and chest that supply the brain and ensures rapid blood loss. The animal bleeds to death. Meat not produced in this way is not considered to be saleable.

Chickens are lifted by their heads until they are immersed in electrified water baths so they can be electrically stunned and become unconscious, but many try to get free and the stunning fails. Chickens and pigs are put in scalding hot water to get rid of their hair and feathers. Sometimes they are still conscious as this happens.

Chickens are usually killed by a mechanical cutter in an assembly line to speed up the process. This is done when they are hanging upside down by their legs on metal shackles on a moving conveyor belt. Chickens can also be gassed to death, as can hens and turkeys.

FACT
There are new techniques that would stun and kill an animal at the same time, but few abattoirs (slaughterhouses use them).

Religious exemptions to the UK law
*There are religious exceptions to the UK law on stunning that makes it compulsory to stun all animals before they are killed for food –

*Animals intended to be eaten by Muslims and Jews don't have to be stunned first.
It used to be the case that animals destined to be halal meat weren't stunned first, but that has changed and an estimated 90% of animals are stunned.

*In order for meat to be considered halal (for Muslims) and Shechita (for Jews) the exposed necks of animals are cut with a sharp knife.

*The ritual slaughter of animals with a knife is justified on religious grounds (Muslims are not allowed to consume blood or 'dead meat', and claim pre-stunning will prevent the entire animal's blood from draining away) and on the assertion that the animal becomes unconscious immediately and feels no pain. Footage of ritual slaughter taken by PETA found that animals were in pain and took as long as three minutes to die.

*For meat to be suitable for followers of Judaism, the animals can't be stunned first as the animal must be healthy before Jews can eat it. But, a pre-cut stun is becoming more commonplace – only in the case of cows and sheep, but not for birds. This means the animals are stunned and right away they have their throats cut.

*Animals that are not stunned are fully conscious as they bleed out and are fully aware of their surroundings.

FACT
Under European law, meat that is halal or Kosher must be labeled. This is to allow consumers to decide whether they want to eat it or not.

FACT
In the UK, there was public outrage when it emerged that people had unwittingly eaten halal meat when they dined out, ate at public events and bought meat from the supermarket. People were angry because they weren't made aware of this and weren't given the choice of whether to eat the meat or not.

Vegetarians & food labeling
In America and the UK, foods tend to be labeled as being suitable for vegetarians or vegans. In other countries like Australia and Germany people are not so lucky. Knowing what to eat can mean scouring the list of ingredients (see **Hidden nasties in our food** later on in this chapter for things to look out for).

TIP
Some companies like *Nestle* have free from lists that tell you which products are suitable for vegetarians, vegans and those with allergies. Visit company websites for details. Look for suitable for vegetarians list, nutritional information or dietary information.

America

Under American law, most ingredients must be listed on the label. Meat must be listed if it appears as a stand-alone ingredient, but the problem for vegetarians and vegans, is that under the definition of **natural flavor**, manufactures can mask a variety of meat-derived products. This includes meat derivatives like chicken and fish stock, poultry, seafood and dairy products that may be used to flavor or bulk up products.

Products may also be labeled as vegan or vegetarian even if they were made in an environment with animal derived products risking the chance of cross contamination.

FACT

Food makers only have to label suitable products as vegan or vegetarian if they want to. They are under no legal obligation to do so.

FACT

The Food Ingredient Right to Know Act, which would have made it easier for vegetarians to identify friendly foods, was launched in 2009. Under the proposal, foods would have to name any flavoring, or coloring derived from meat, poultry, or other animal products (including insects) on the label under a new amended amend *Federal Food, Drug and Cosmetic Act*. The bill ran out of time.

FACT

The American Vegetarian Association has an AVA Certified logo, which clearly shows whether products are vegetarian, or vegan.

TIP

Just because a product carries a meat free label does not mean it's suitable for vegetarians. It may contain slaughterhouse byproducts like gelatin or fish.

The UK

There is no legal definition for vegetarian in the UK or the European Union. The Vegetarian Society in the UK want there to be because at the moment foods can carry a suitable for vegetarians or a simple V symbol and contain battery farmed eggs. Most vegetarians only eat free-range eggs.

Note, foods that have *the Vegetarian Society* approved green V logo (in the UK) are made from free-range eggs. Quorn products also carry this logo. This is the most trusted vegetarian logo.

Stores also have their own suitable for vegetarian labeling on their products, whether it's wording such as vegetarian, which usually appears down from the list of ingredients and near where a warning to say nut allergy sufferers is printed. Or, it can appear on the front of the packaging as either a V symbol or in word form suitable for vegetarians, near the nutritional breakdown, including amount of calories contained in the product.

FACT

Sadly, very few foodstuffs are labeled as being suitable for vegans, even when products are. In those cases, as a consumer you are faced with two options – not to buy, or to scrutinize the ingredients themselves. Seeing a vegetarian logo at least means there's a chance a product is vegan friendly.

Foods labeled as suitable for vegetarians or vegans are, however, subject to provisions within the *Trades Descriptions Act 1968.*

In 2006, *the Food Standards Agency in the UK* (FSA) published guidance aimed at improving food labeling for vegans and vegetarians. The Vegetarian Society and the Vegan Society were consulted along with other shareholders. For the first time, criteria for the use of terms vegetarian and vegan on food labels was established.

This states the term vegetarian should not be applied to "foods that are, or are made from or with the aid of, products derived from animals that have died, have been slaughtered, or animals that die as a result of being eaten. Animals means farmed, wild or domestic animals, including for example, livestock, poultry, game, fish, shellfish, crustaceans, amphibians, tunicates, echinoderms, mollusks* and insects." – Source, *Foods Standard Agency* (UK) website at www.food.gov.uk

* spelt mollusk in America, this refers to over a thousand creatures which have soft bodies that are usually protected by shells, like shellfish, squids, scallops, snails, mussels, clams etc…

The Food Standards Agency also states – 'The term vegan should not be applied to foods that are, or are made from or with the aid of animals or animal products (including products from living animals).'

In addition, manufacturers, retailers and caterers of products labeled vegetarian or vegan, also have to show that foods labeled in this way have not been contaminated with non-vegetarian or vegan products when they were made, prepared or stored. If there's a chance of this the label must carry a warning along the lines of "this was prepared in a factory making meat/fish products."

FACT

The Vegan logo is a registered trademark that shows items that bear it have met vegan animal free standards.*
Source – *The Vegan Society* website.

FACT

The town of Ghent in Belgium is the first place in the world to have a weekly vegetarian day. This began in 2009 on a Thursday, and is now on the same day every week. On the day, selected civil servants and councilors will eat vegetarian meals. This is being done to highlight the impact meat consumption has on the environment.

"One of the most effective things any individual can do to help the environment is to eat less meat."
Paul McCartney

Myths about vegetarianism

There are so many myths and misconceptions about vegetarianism.

Perhaps the most common one is that vegetarians are skinny and pale looking because they don't get the iron the human body gets from eating meat.

Certainly meat is one of the highest sources of iron. But, there are many more things that have high iron contents that don't come from dead animals –

*Sesame seeds have a higher iron count than most meats. They can also be eaten in a variety of ways – on their own, in salads or in bread.

*Cashew nuts are a good source of iron. Ideally with no salt.

*Dried fruits like apricots, prunes and raisins.

*Beans. Lima beans in particular have a high iron content.

*Green leafy vegetables like spinach and lettuce.

*Dark chocolate.

*Whole grains such as popcorn, brown or wild rice, whole grain breads, quinoa and Bulgar wheat.

*Curry powder. High in iron, the only trouble is that generally we don't eat a lot of it.

*In addition, vegetarian friendly iron is added to all breakfast cereals and some bread.
Cereals can also have iron added and there are supplements available.

TIP
Having something containing vitamin C at the same time as a food with iron, helps the body to absorb iron. Avoid having anything that interferes with the body absorbing iron at the same time as you have something with iron. This means no caffeine, no milk and soy (Soya) although it contains an easily absorbed iron; it also contains a substance that can lower the body's iron absorption rate).

There are many other myths about vegetarians too. Some of the most common are –

MYTH - If we all stopped eating meat, farm animals would die out.

Animals are being bred in their masses for food. If more people decided to stop eating meat, there simply wouldn't be as many animals being bred by man just to be eaten.

MYTH - Eating meat is manly.
This goes back to the days when man was the hunter-gatherer whilst the women stayed at home. The implication with this view is that choosing to be a compassionate human being somehow dilutes someone's manliness. In response to this, vegetarians and vegans could politely point out there is nothing vaguely macho about eating a domesticated animal that has been farmed and then killed by someone else for them to eat.

MYTH - You need meat to survive.
Millions of vegetarians the world over are proof that is simply not true. This idea comes from the belief that all humans need protein and you can only get that from meat. Yet protein can come from a number of plant sources like bananas, tofu, soybeans (the richest source of plant protein), Seitan* (pronounced say- tahn, but also called gluten in America and wheat meat), Quorn (not vegan as it contains eggs), gardein (available in America and Canada only and suitable for vegans) and nuts and seeds.
*Seitan is a low fat, high protein meat alternative that comes from the protein part of wheat. It's not suitable for anyone with a gluten intolerance. It has been used for thousands of years in the Middle East, Asia and Russia.

MYTH - It's not healthy for children to be vegetarian
At a time when many children are vastly overweight because of meat-laden convenience foods and not eating enough fruit and vegetables, how can a diet that is rich in fruit and vegetables possibly be detrimental to their health? As long as all dietary requirements are met, children who grow up not eating meat are generally healthier than those who eat meat, because they eat so much more of the good stuff.

Hidden nasties in our food

There are ingredients in our food that at first glance you would assume were cruelty free, but you'd be wrong -

Animal Rennet
Most vegetarians do eat dairy products like milk and cheese because no animal had to die to produce these two products, but vegans abstain from all animal products, so they don't any dairy.

Not all cheeses are suitable for vegetarians because they may contain animal rennet. There is no such thing as cruelty free animal rennet. It's produced from the stomach lining of killed baby calves. Yet synthetic rennet can be used instead. This is usually used in vegetarian cheese.

Animal rennet may also be present in some potato chips (crisps) and cheese type sauces.

The good news is that most supermarket cheeses in America, Canada and the UK are suitable for vegetarians, but unless a cheese is labeled as vegetarian or **suitable for vegetarians** or **containing/made with vegetable rennet**, it's not vegetarian.

TIP

When eating out, if you want to eat cruelty free (vegetarian) cheese, it's best to ask what kind of cheese they use. You have every right to know what you're about to eat. Most cheese these days is vegetarian, but you should always check.

Cochineal

This is normally used in foods that need a reddish/pinkish and orange coloring, but is also used in cosmetics. It's made by picking the insects off cacti before killing them in hot water and then drying and pulverizing their bodies.

It can also be down on the label as carmine, Carminic Acid, Carmines Natural Red 4 and E120, which is the name of the dye extracted from the insects' bodies and eggs. Fears over artificial dyes have led to the increased use of this dye, which was first used in 15th century South American, but carmine can cause asthma in some people and hyperactivity in children

FACT

The British based *Hyperactive Children's Support Group*, recommend that cochineal should be eliminated from the diet of hyperactive children.
See www.hacsg.org.uk for details.

Many Muslims consider carmine-containing food haram (forbidden) because the dye is extracted from insects, and Jewish people also avoid foodstuffs containing this additive.

Cochineal and carmine can be found in meat, poultry, sausages, soft drinks, alcohol, cakes and pastries as a topping, preserves, desserts and sweets.

As of January 5th, 2011, the *U.S. Food and Drug Administration* regulation require all foods and cosmetics containing cochineal to declare it on their ingredient labels. This is because of health concerns over the substance.

Gelatin (spelt gelatine in the UK)
This is made by boiling the bones, skin and tendons of animals' bones and is most commonly used in jello (jelly in the UK), marshmallows, jelly type candies (sweets) like Jelly Babies and some low fat yoghurts and desserts like dessert. It can also be used in some soft drinks to disperse the color.

Gelatin can be bought in the form of granules, powder and sheets for household use, usually in baking as a gelling agent.

Gelatin's E number is **441** and it's a byproduct of the meat and leather industry. It comes mainly from cows and pigs. In the UK, most gelatin is beef in origin. This makes it unsuitable for vegetarians and vegans.

TIP
There are many alternatives to gelatin. The two most commonly used are, gar-agar (it comes from seaweed and is used to make vegetarian marshmallows) and pectin (it usually is derived from citrus fruits).

FACT
Most medicine and vitamin capsules are also made of gelatin, but liquid forms of the medicines that are free of the substance may be available. For instance, the antidepressant Prozac comes in gelatin shells, but can also be taken in pure liquid form.

Glycerin/Glycerol (Glycerine in the UK)

This can come from animal fat, but you can also get vegetarian glycerin. Unless a product specifically states it is vegetable in origin, its wise to assume it's of the animal variety. If in any doubt, ask the manufacturer as companies do not always put the source of the glycerin on the label.

Products that can contain animal glycerin, are soap, cosmetics, toothpastes, and some foods like candies (sweets as they call them in the UK).

TIP

Coconut and palm oils are popular sources of vegetable glycerin.

Isinglass

You get this from the swim bladder of a fish and it's used as a filtering agent in drinks, both alcoholic and non-alcoholic. The final drink does not contain isinglass as it's for filtering only, but the fact the fish have to be dead first to get their bladders makes anything filtered with isinglass not suitable for vegans and vegetarians.

Isinglass is used in the production of *Guinness*, *Lilt* (in the UK) and many other alcoholic beverages.

Please note – This is by no means an exhaustive guide and some of the products mentioned that are not suitable for vegetarians at the time this was printed may have stopped using animal products.

Lard

Lard is animal fat and as such isn't suitable for vegetarian or vegans. It used to be popular in the UK as a spread on bread. These days, it can be found mainly in cakes, biscuits and desserts.

TIP
Mincemeat and suet may contain lard, but there are vegetarian alternatives to both and as people become more health conscious, lard is no longer as popular as it once was.

Vitamin D
Cereals are often fortified with this vitamin, which helps to keep bones strong. This vitamin is unusual as you can also get it from sun exposure. But, vegans need to be wary as often vitamin D comes from sheep's wool (this is called D3 or cholecalciferol).

There are vegan suitable supplements of vitamin D available, which come from yeast or mushrooms. When sourced from plant material, it's called D2. Vitamin D is often added to soy (Soya) milk. A deficiency in this vitamin has been linked to cancer and most people don't get enough of the sunshine vitamin.

Things that don't sound vegetarian but they are

When you are a vegetarian or a vegan, it can be a nightmare trying to figure out whether something is okay to eat.

Cheese
Most cheeses these days do not contain animal rennet. Instead they use a non-animal version that requires no animals to be used. Nowadays, there are also vegan cheeses available that are made without milk.

Meat flavored potato chips (crisps)
Of all the questions vegetarians get this is one of the most common – "can you eat meat flavored potato chips?"

Many people believe that flavor from real meat is used to flavor potato chips, but that isn't always the case. Most flavorings come from artificial sources or from vegetables. For instance, bacon flavored chips may be flavored with beetroot juice. The main type of chips vegetarians need to be on the look out for are cheese flavored ones, because animal rennet might have been used. Fishy flavors should also be avoided although prawn cocktail flavors are usually artificial.

FACT
In the UK, crisp company Walkers caused a storm of protest when they decided to use real meat in their crisps. Smoky bacon, a long-time favorite of vegetarians, is now no longer suitable for vegetarians as it contains real meat. So too does their chicken flavor and cheese and onion is also often made with animal rennet.

FACT
If you're vegetarian and want to eat a packet of cheesy snacks, make sure the product is suitable for vegetarians. Many cheesy snacks contain genuine animal rennet from the guts of calves and not the synthetic kind.

Pregelatinized starch
Vegetarians and vegans don't eat gelatin (also spelt gelatine), so seeing this on a label can be a cause for concern. But, this doesn't contain gelatin at all. In fact, it usually comes from maize that has been cooked and dried.

Pregelatinized starch is commonly found in the capsules medicines and vitamins come in to make them suitable for different diets.

Whey

This is one of those tricky ingredients you'll find, sitting somewhere in the middle of the list, usually in chocolate products. Whey most often comes from the cheese making process where animal rennet is used, so is not suitable for vegetarians never mind vegans. It's also used in some potato chips (crisps in the UK). Unless it specifies that it comes from cow's milk, whey is not suitable for vegetarians or vegans because to get it involves killing a calf.

TIP

Be wary of products that say they contain "no artificial colorings, flavorings and preservatives." Often they contain slaughterhouse by-products like whey (from a dead baby calf's stomach) or cochineal (made from crushed insects).

Worcester sauce

This contains anchovies, which are small fish. The good news is there are vegetarian/vegan versions available. Check the label.

The lowdown on vegetarianism & veganism

1. Vegetarians don't eat any animal flesh. This includes meat, fish and chicken. Outwith India, most vegetarians do eat dairy and eggs.

2. Vegans don't eat any animal products. This includes things that don't result in an animal being killed like honey and beeswax. They also don't wear wool or leather.

3. The majority of vegetarians choose their lifestyle because of ethical concerns over animal welfare. There are also people who are vegetarian because of their religious beliefs.

4. There is no legal definition for vegetarian in the UK or America.

5. There is no legal obligation for foods that are suitable for vegetarians to say that on the label.

6. There are hidden slaughterhouse by-products in foodstuffs, so it's always best to check the label. If still in doubt, contact the manufacturer.

7. If you want to ensure a food is suitable for vegetarians or vegans, check the label for the approved symbol. To be completely sure, check the ingredients carefully.

8. The myth that all vegetarians and vegans are pale looking and thin isn't true and the diets are known for their health properties.

"The vegetarian food market has been growing for decades. Although the number of committed vegetarians has remained stable in recent years, the number of meat-reducers has increased enormously."
The Vegetarian Society (UK's) head of communications, Liz O'Neill.

Chapter 5
Meat reducers

It used to be the case that those who didn't eat meat were defined as either vegetarians or vegans. In recent years, a new group has emerged - the meat reducers.

In *the Vegetarian Times* magazine survey conducted in 2008, it was found that 22.8million people lived a "vegetarian inclined" lifestyle, meaning they were actively trying to eat less meat.

Meat reducers can be people who want to become vegetarian eventually and find it difficult, or they may not want to give up eating meat completely. They may want to cut down, often for health reasons, because meat is bad for you and rarely a week goes by without the medical profession and scientists telling us we need to eat less meat and more fruit and vegetables.

FACT
In 2010, *The Guardian* newspaper in the UK reported that the number of high-end vegetarian restaurants was rising because of health and environmental concerns over eating meat.

FACT
In 2008, the UN recommended that people should have one meat-free day if they wanted to make a difference to climate change. The UN's *Food and Agriculture Organization* estimated that meat production accounted for nearly a fifth of global greenhouse gas emissions. Much of this was down to cows emitting methane gasses and the resources taken up to producing enough for the cows to eat.

Meat reducers don't want to give up eating meat completely. They want to cut down, usually for health reasons, because rarely a week goes by without the medical profession and scientists telling us we need to eat less meat and more fruit and vegetables.

Who are the meat reducers?

Meat reducers tend to fall into two camps –
They want to reduce the amount of all meats they consume for health reasons. They may be worried about heart disease, putting on weight, or worry they could "catch" Bird Flu or *Mad cow disease (bovine spongiform encephalopathy) which originated in the UK.

They want to stop eating red meat like steak because they think its bad for them. They will probably eat white leaner meats like chicken and turkey instead.

*What's mad cow disease?
Mad cow disease or BSE (bovine spongiform encephalopathy) is a progressive and lethal central nervous system disease in cows that is believed to be manmade. Scientists can tell its present if they see clear holes in the brains of cows. These holes look like sponge and that's where spongiform came from.

Scientists believe that BSE was created after cows, who are vegetarian animals, were fed sheep offal (the leftover parts of killed sheep that are considered unfit for human consumption). When the animals died, they in turn were put into feed for other animals to eat which accelerated the spread of the disease.

At its height in the 90's, millions of cows were culled (slaughtered) in the UK and there was a ban on exporting British beef.

The human strain of mad cow disease is called *Variant Creutzfeldt-Jakob disease* (vCJD) and was first diagnosed in the mid-1990's. Humans contracted it through eating infected beef. It causes neurological problems - usually starting with behavioral changes, insomnia and lack of coordination – and progresses to the patient being unable to talk or move until eventually they lapse into a coma and die.

At the moment, there is no cure and scientists believe that the disease may be lying dormant in many more people and some of them may have been wrongly diagnosed with Alzheimer's, Huntingdon's or dementia, which have similar symptoms.

FACT
The disease can lay dormant in cows and humans and can only be conclusively diagnosed after death by dissecting the brain.

The ethical meat refusers
There is a third group who want to cut down their meat consumption. They're not doing it for health reasons or because they think certain meats are bad for them. They have moral objections to eating certain types of meat.

Maybe because of what animal the meat came from, or because of how the animal was treated before it died. This may include things like Foie gras (see **Chapter.2 - Things that can never be cruelty free**), venison, duck and exotic types of meats like ostrich. They may object to eating certain animals like rabbit, squirrel, kangaroo and shark.

"I would recommend to people to control their consumption of meat to maintain a healthy weight and good health in general during life."
Researcher Dr Anne-Claire Vergnaud

Why eating less meat is good for you
There are many solid, scientific reasons why cutting down on meat can improve your health and your chances of getting certain diseases –

1. Most meats tends to be higher in fat than plant protein which means you are at a higher risk of heart disease if you eat meat, especially fatty meats like steak.
Meat can be high in calories. Vegetarians tend to be slimmer than their meat-eating counterparts.

2. Meat is harder for the human body to digest than plant protein, which may explain the findings of a European study of 400,000 people that found that the people who ate meat put on more weight than those who didn't, even when they were consuming the same amount of calories.

3. Meat is high in saturated fat, which has been linked with breast and bowel cancer.
Those who eat meat regularly are less likely than their vegetarian counterparts to eat enough fruit and vegetables.

4. You're more likely to get food poisoning if you eat meat, especially during barbecue season.

5. You can reduce your cancer risk by cutting down on meat consumption. This may be down to a number of things – the slowness with which meat passes through your body, the drugs the animals you eat were given to fatten them up quicker and the fact that plants have cancer fighting nutrients and plenty of fiber, amongst others.

FACT
In 2009, a US study featured in Archives of Internal Medicine, found that those who consumed large quantities of meat had an increased risk of death from all causes including cancer and heart disease. The study was conducted over ten years and 500,000 people took part.

Farm animal welfare
One of the reasons people are eating less meat is over animal welfare concerns especially in light of traditionally farming methods being replaced by factory farming. These days we're more interested in where our food comes from.

There are organizations devoted to promoting the welfare of farm animals –

In America, The Humane Society of the United States (HSUS), works to improve the conditions of farm animals. They believe the three components of humane eating are reduce, replace and refine.

Reduce as in reducing the amount of animal products consumed.
Refine as in refining the diet to eat less products from the cruelest production systems like veal (made by placing calves in crates) and Foie gras (made by force-feeding ducks and geese).

Replace as in replacing animal products like meat in your diet with plant foods.

The Humane Society of the United States doesn't simply promote vegetarianism or going vegan, they also promote what's known as *flexitarianism*. Flexitarians limit the amount of meat they eat and are like meat reducers. They often cut down on meat for health reasons. They may not eat meat on certain days or only eat meat for certain meals, say none for lunch but some for dinner.

Note - Flexitarians have been labeled "part-time vegetarians," but this is not accurate. Vegetarianism is a everyday thing and not something you can be part-time.

Read more about the HSUS by visiting their website at www.humanesociety.org

Canada
The Animal Welfare Foundation of Canada (The AWC) works towards improving the welfare of animals throughout the country whether they are companion animals (pets) or farm animals. One of the ways they do this is by offering grants for projects that improve animal welfare.

Visit their website at www.awfc.ca

Canadian Coalition for Farm Animals (CCFA) also campaigns for farm animals to be treated more humanely. See www.humanefood.ca

South Africa

Animal Voice is the mouthpiece for *Compassion in World Farming* (South Africa). They campaign against unconscionable practices on farm animals. They have a monthly magazine called Animal Voice. See www.animal-voice.org

Australia

Animals Australia campaigns against live animal exports, battery sheep farming and against placing pigs in stalls. They investigate and expose animal cruelty. Read more about their work on their website at www.animalsaustralia.org

The UK

In the UK, crusading *Compassion in World Farming* (CiWF) are the main charity. They were set up by dairy farmer Peter Roberts in 1967 after he became concerned about the welfare of animals in modern industrial type farms. They believe factory farming is the biggest cause of animal cruelty on the planet. Read more about them by visiting their website www.ciwf.org.uk

Worldwide

PETA also campaigns for farm animals throughout the world. For details of their work visit www.peta.org
Go to the search box on the top of the screen on the right hand side and enter say farm animals or chicken to find out more. Please be warned, there may be disturbing images on the site.

Note – They also have a site especially aimed at children. Click on PETA kids on the top right of the page.

FACT
Even if you have no moral objections to eating animals, many people do care about how animals are treated prior to their deaths because poorly fed and treated animals who are terrified before they are killed produce poor quality meat.

"Factory farming systems deprive the animals of everything that makes life worth living."
Peter Roberts MBE (founder of Compassion in World Farming)

Is there such a thing as more humane meat?
Yes. In the old days we had meat that was more humane than it is now. That's because farm animals were raised outside and had the freedom to roam, but with the huge increase in the world's population, factory farming became the new way to farm animals. This was done for one reason only – to make as much money as possible from as much meat as possible. To do this, animal welfare fell by the wayside.

Animals were given hormones to make them grow fat faster. They were kept in small stalls and deprived of contact with their own kind. They were fed as little as possible to keep feeding costs down and given food that it wasn't natural for them to eat. For instance, vegetarian cows were made to eat bone meal made out of the remains of other cattle. Going against nature had the consequence of creating infections like Mad Cow Disease, which transferred to humans after they ate contaminated beef.

Nowadays, with the spotlight on more humane meat, it is possible to get meat from animals who were treated more humanely, although it must be stressed that no meat is cruelty free -

The Certified Humane Raised and Handled label ® (USA)
This is backed by *the Humane Society of the US* and the
American Society for the Prevention of Cruelty to Animals
(ASPCA). Having the label guarantees that the animals killed
to produce the food were treated humanely from the day they
were born until they were killed. This means they were raised
with enough space to behave in a natural way, are not given
antibiotics and hormones and most importantly, cages, crates
and tie stalls are completely banned if a producer wants to
qualify for the label.

Read more about it by visiting their website
www.certifiedhumane.org

Note – the label is often shortened to American Humane
Certified.

Freedom Food (UK)
In England and Wales, the Royal Society for the Prevention of
Cruelty to Animals (RSPCA) runs the Freedom Food scheme.
Its aim is to improve the welfare of all animals reared for food.
Every farmer who applies to have the label on their produce
must meet standards set by the RSPCA and must also agree to
be assessed. They will also be visited by a Freedom Food
inspector once every year.

Find out more at the website at
www.rspca.org.uk/freedomfood

Freedom Foods can be bought in many major UK
supermarkets and stores like Tesco, Sainsbury's, Morrisons,
the Co-Op and Waitrose.

Note – In Scotland, *the Freedom Food* scheme is overseen by an independent organization called Scottish Food Quality Certification. This is because Scotland has its own version of the *RSPCA*, *the Scottish Society for the Prevention of Cruelty to Animals* (SSPCA) which is a completely different organization to the *RSPCA*.

"I'm not a vegetarian, but I have cut back sharply on the meat that I eat."
Al Gore

How to reduce the amount of meat in your diet
The easiest way to do this is to have a meat free day (see below). One day a week when the whole family don't eat meat. A number of family favorites can be adapted to be completely free of meat.

What to have on meat free days
Have a veggie roast - Instead of having a Sunday Roast or the traditional Thanksgiving meat feast, vegetarians can have a nut roast or a chicken, turkey or beef (flavored) Quorn roast, which are just as tasty. The veggie equivalents also contain a lot less calories than the traditional roast. Quorn is also low in fat and fills you up and it's tasty. Quorn is lower in calories than meat and high in protein. And, at a time when we're all being warned about having high cholesterol (it can be a precursor to heart disease and a raft of other ailments like heart attacks), Quorn has zero cholesterol.

See their website at www.quorn.co.uk for more details. Of all vegetarian foods, Quorn is one of the most widely available.

Note – Just as some people have food intolerances or allergies to things like nuts and shellfish, people can also have a reaction to Quorn.

Spaghetti Bolognese can be made by adding Soy, TVP (textured vegetable protein) or Quorn mince to the spaghetti. The same mince can also be used to make one of Scotland's traditional dishes, stovies. Just add veggie sausages, potatoes and carrot and onion gravy and hey presto, you have a tasty meal without the high fat and calories.

How about some **pasta**? Easy to make and very filling, you can add whatever sauce you like or try making your own using fresh tomatoes and herbs. Very tasty and easy to make.

Have a veggie salad. You can have all the vegetables that you want, but instead of the usual ham or tuna, why not try a meat substitute like Quorn or tofu or one of the many mock meats available?

Baked potatoes and potato skins are simple to make and you can add any topping you want. Why not have baked beans or cheese and pickle or a nice salad?

Many of the vegetarian brands these days have their own fishless products like fishless fish cakes and mock tuna. Have that instead of your usual fish. Remember that over-fishing is one of the causes of climate change.

How about having fun as a family and making your own pizza? You can buy the base from a store or make your own using dough. Add things like peppers, peppercorns, sweetcorn, olives, onions, cheese, tomato, carrot, grilled or fried eggplant (aubergines in the UK), nuts, herbs, artichokes, red peppers, herbs, garlic and zucchini (courgettes). The only limit is your imagination. Your homemade pizza is guaranteed to taste delicious like everything does when you make it yourself.

Have some **vegetarian or vegan hot dogs**. It's not just vegetarians who say they taste better than the meat version, which is usually made from mechanically separated meat: the poorest quality of meat.

Curries are fantastic too. There are so many variations and traditionally in India where curries originate from, meat is rarely used because many people are Hindus (most of whom are vegetarian) or the meat is such poor quality that no one eats it.

And, if its fast food you want, why not **ditch the Big Mac for a tasty veggie burger**. You can get all kinds: spicy, nutty, hot, sweet or regular.

TIP
If you decide that vegetarianism is for you, you can start off as a meat reducer and change your diet gradually. But, if you feel like you could never ditch meat permanently, you can still make a real difference (to your health and the planet) by not eating meat one day of the week or shunning cruel foods like lobster, veal, venison (baby deer) and Foie gras.

Considering going vegetarian or vegan?

There are so many free and helpful resources on the Internet for you. If you want advice on how to live a vegetarian lifestyle, or even on how to cut down on your meat consumption, these sites can help –

www.americanvegan.org *The American Vegan Society* (AVS) Their site explains more about the vegan lifestyle. They have a quarterly subscriber only magazine, aptly called American Vegan.

www.americanvegetarian.org (*The American Vegetarian Society*) - Their site has a list of verified vegetarian products on their home page.

www.navs-online.org (*The North American Vegetarian Society NAVS*) - Founded in 1974, they want to not only offer advice to vegetarians in America and Canada, but to also educate people about vegetarianism. They founded World Vegetarian Day, which is celebrated on October 1st every year. They have a section on frequently asked questions, as well as tasty recipe ideas. On their site, down the left hand side, they have helpful topics like FAQ, Food and recipes and Dining Out.

www.vegsoc.org (*The Vegetarian Society UK*). Established in 1847, they are the oldest vegetarian organization in the world. They aim to educate people about vegetarianism and to support vegetarians. They have a comprehensive advice and information section. On the home page, you can click on a number of options, including Info & Advice and Go Veggie & Why.

www.vegansociety.com (*The Vegan Society*). The best place to go for advice on going vegan. Click on the cloud on the left hand side that reads 'Become a vegan' of the home page. They also produce an Animal Free Shopper. See home page and half way down Animal Free Shopper.

www.viva.org.uk (*Viva!* are *Vegetarians International Voice for Animals*). Their website has advice on going veggie including animal free recipes, as well as details of campaigns to improve animal welfare. They have menus for **Going vegetarian and Going Vegan** on the left hand side menu on the home page.

http://veg-soc.org *The Australian Vegetarian Society* has a free book available for download on their site called Go Vegetarian. You can also join them and receive the quarterly member's magazine Health and Vegetarian Life.

http://www.vegetarian.org.nz/content *The New Zealand Vegetarian Society* offers advice on how to live meat and fish free. You can send for a free information pack via their site.

*"I am not interested to know whether vivisection produces
results that are profitable to the human race or doesn't...The
pain which it inflicts upon un-consenting animals is the basis
of my enmity toward it, and it is to me sufficient justification
of the enmity without looking further."*
Mark Twain

Chapter 6
Cruelty Free Cosmetics

The testing of cosmetics on animals has always been a very
conscientious issue. On one hand, there are those who say that
unless this testing is carried out, cosmetics will not be safe for
human use, and humans should come first before animals.

On the other hand, there are those who insist that there is no
need to test products like foundation and perfumes on
animals because it's cruel and unethical. They also argue that
cosmetics are for vanity reasons and are not essential.

It is the second opinion, which seems to be the most popular
even amongst people who are not vegetarian or vegan. So
popular in fact, that in 2013 in the European Union, most
cosmetics testing were banned.

America will not be following suit, although there have been
calls for them to adopt the same ban, by animal welfare
charities such as *The American Anti-vivisection Society* and
PETA.

In a 2010 a *YouGov* poll conducted in the UK, 60% of those asked said they didn't think cosmetics should be tested on animals.

Animal testing & the law

America

Cosmetics testing used to be unregulated in America until 1938 when congress gave the *FDA* (*The Food and Drug Administration*) the right to regulate cosmetics. For the purposes of the 1938 Act, cosmetics were defined as products for "cleansing, beautifying, promoting attractiveness, or altering the appearance."

This was in no small part due to an incident that took place in 1933 in the country. Women used mascara called **Lush Lure**, which was supposed to make their lashes look darker. The product worked, but had catastrophic side effects. Some women suffered from eye irritation, whilst others were blinded and one person died.

The side effects were attributed to paraphenylenediamine, a chemical extremely toxic to the body, which was used as the dyeing agent in the mascara. However, after this substance was found to be toxic it would no longer be used.

FACT
There is currently no legal requirement for cosmetics to be tested on animals in America. They do however have a duty for companies to prove that their products aren't toxic or pose a threat to public safety. This can be done without animal testing.

Canada

There is no legal obligation to test cosmetics on animals. For the purposes of the law, cosmetics are defined as "a product which cleanses, improves or alters the complexion, skin, hair or teeth."

Australia

It's illegal to test cosmetics on animals in Australia, but this doesn't mean all cosmetics on sale are cruelty free. To get round the no testing law, companies have their products tested abroad in countries like China. This is a common situation worldwide where a country will ban animal testing on cosmetics in their own country, but not ban the importing of animal tested products.

For more information the ban on testing cosmetics on animals in Australia, visit www.animalsaustralia.org/take_action/ban-animal-tested-products

The UK

The testing of products and ingredients on animals was banned in the UK in 1998.

However, this is not to say that after 1998, all cosmetics bought in the UK have not been tested on animals, or had their ingredients tested on animals. There are still cosmetics on sale in the UK that have been tested on animals. These tests have been done outside the UK. This is the loophole many companies use to beat the ban.

FACT
The bulk of animal cosmetics testing, these days, is carried out in China where labor is cheap and there are few laws governing animal welfare. In China, all cosmetics that are sold in China must undergo animal testing. This includes products made out with China that are exported. For this reason, The Body Shop will not be exporting its products to China. In 2014, they removed all of their products from Chinese airports because the products were at risk of being tested on animals.

The European Union ban
In March 2013, the EU wide ban on cosmetics testing on animals came into force. This followed the 2009 legislation, which implemented a partial ban on the sale anywhere in the EU of cosmetics and toiletries containing ingredients, which have been tested on animals.

According to *the BUAV* - "The 2013 ban means that companies are no longer able to animal test new cosmetic products and ingredients on sale in the EU. However, companies can still carry on animal testing cosmetics outside the EU where these cosmetics are also sold outside the EU. There are a number of issues for companies selling their products on the global market. For example, at present, before new products can go on sale in China, they must be submitted for testing to the Chinese authorities, which normally involves a range of animal tests."

FACT
The leaping Bunny logo is still the only label that you can trust to be completely cruelty free as companies who earn the logo are thoroughly vetted.

"The EU has banned all animal tests for cosmetic ingredients, formulations, and final products. In addition, the sale of cosmetics and ingredients that have been tested on animals, regardless of where the testing occurred, is also prohibited, with the exception of three test areas (repeated-dose toxicity, reproductive toxicity, and toxicokinetics). The final three test areas will be banned in March 2013."
Source – The EU website

What tests are conducted on animals?

The most common tests carried out on animals are –

Draize Skin Tests
In this test, animals such as rabbits, mice and rats have their fur shaved and then they have the cosmetic product like shampoo or make up rubbed into the area.

Why they do this: to see if there is any damage or irritation to the area. This is meant to predict how the product will react on human skin.

Why anti-vivisectionists oppose this:
1. It's cruel and causes unnecessary pain and suffering to the animals used.

2. It will not predict how the product will react in humans.

3. On most products it will say not to use on irritated or broken skin.

Draize Eye Tests
Of all animal tests for cosmetics, these are considered the cruelest.

White albino rabbits are used because they are unable to wash away irritable substances from their eyes. Their heads are immobilized, so they cannot move and then different chemicals are dripped into their eyes and left there to see how their eyes react. Researchers then check their eyes for any irritation or damage.

This test is used for both cosmetics and household products like washing powder and bleach, and was devised because of the Lush Lure incident.

Why they do this: like the skin test, any damage or irritation to the area is recorded. This is meant to predict how the product will react in human eyes.

Why anti-vivisectionists oppose this:
1. There is a huge difference between the eyes of rabbits and humans. For instance, we produce a lot more tears than the rabbits used in these tests that are chosen specifically because they produce so few tears.

2. The tests are painful for the rabbits who are given no form of pain relief.
Animals unlike humans, cannot tell you how they are feeling.

3. The contraptions used to confine the rabbits to keep them still are like some form of medieval torture device.

3. **Lethal Dose Tests (LD 50 Tests)**
Animals are force-fed substances (usually by having a tube forced down their throats) or they are injected with them, or made to inhale them to see just how much will kill them LF50 stands for the lethal dose it will take to kill 50 percent of the test subjects. Animals usually vomit, suffer convulsions, are paralyzed and have bleeding from the skin, nose, eyes and mouth.

Why they do this: To evaluate how toxic something is and to hopefully relate that data to humans.

Why anti-vivisectionists oppose this:
1. It's a horrific and painful way for animals to die.

2. It does not guarantee what the lethal dose is in humans who will react in a different way as we are genetically different. Not to mention much larger.

3. The tests don't result in safer products. Often personal care products that carry warnings about causing skin irritation and allergic reactions are still made available for sale, which makes you wonder why they bother to put animals through grueling tests to find that out.

Is it possible to test products safely without using animals?

In a word, yes. A number of tests have been developed. The development of these tests is very important as they can also be used to test drugs and other chemicals. This speeds up research.

Here are the most commonly used ones -

1. PETA (People for the Ethical Treatment of Animals) helped fund the development of the cruelty-free skin irritation test. No animals are used in this test. Instead they are replaced with three-dimensional reconstructions of human skin using cells grown in culture. This test is now widely used and considered to be more accurate and efficient than testing on animals.

2. Human Patch Tests – These are conducted on human volunteers and because of that they are more reliable than animal testing.

In Canada, these tests are conducted on human volunteers who are considered as a valid replacement for skin irritation studies on animals. However skin patch tests are only used after scientists first confirm that chemicals are not corrosive using another non-animal method and various computer modeling and test tube studies to make sure that any patch test done uses chemicals that are not obvious irritants.

3. Eyetex™
Unlike the Draize eye tests, rabbits aren't used; a vegetable dye that reacts to any irritants like the cornea of the human eye is used in their place. This test is considered to be more reliable than the Draize eye test. This is because in the Draize test, people have to estimate the damage caused, meaning results are all down to human error and are not exact. With Eyetex™, more accurate information is obtained because the results can be measured by a machine called a spectrophotometer.

How do you tell if a product is cruelty free?
It has never been easier to buy products that are cruelty free. This is because of the introduction of clear labeling. There are clear logos placed on products that make it clear that these products are not tested on animals and neither are their ingredients -

BUAV
APPROVED

The Leaping Bunny logo

Go to http://www.leapingbunny.org to see what the logo looks like.

Cruelty free products carry what is known as **the Leaping Bunny logo**, which is also known as **The Humane Cosmetics Standard (HCS)** and **Humane Household Products Standard** (HHPS). This is administered by *The Coalition for Consumer Information on Cosmetics* (CCIC) who do onsite checks of any company wishing to use their logo. This logo is recognized In America, Canada, most European countries and the UK.

To earn the right to display this cruelty free standard on their products, the makers of cosmetics, toiletries, baby products and household products, must show that particular product was made without any animal testing and that includes the ingredients, the final product and any stage of its development.

Only companies that are approved, are allowed to carry the famous leaping bunny logo and they get to be listed on both the online and published Compassionate Shopping Guide.

Visit their website at – www.leapingbunny.org for more details.
www.gocrueltyfree.org also carries the same information

The British approved bunny logo
In the UK, products carry the same Leaping Bunny logo with the addition of BUAV approved, which means that neither the ingredients, nor the final product were tested on animals. The BUAV is the British Union for the Abolition of Vivisection. As well as campaigning against all animal testing, they also do undercover investigations and political lobbying.
Visit their website at – www.buav.org for further details.

Any company that has their logo on their products must meet the same strict guidelines as the Leaping Bunny mark. In the UK, all of Superdrug's own brand products carry this logo.

The BUAV also produce the free pocket guide The Little Book of Cruelty Free, listing cruelty free companies who qualify to put their logo on products. It's available to order or to download online at
http://www.gocrueltyfree.org/consumer/get-involved/lbcf-request

TIP
PETA (People for the Ethical Treatment of Animals) provides a list of cruelty free companies on their website at peta.org (they cover US & UK companies, as well as world brands). However, their criteria for being on the list aren't as stringent as the Leaping Bunny ones.

TIP
The Vegan's Society produces **the Animal Free Shopper Guide** for vegans in the UK. Check it out at - www.vegansociety.com

What are fixed cut off dates?
Companies, who carry the Leaping Bunny mark, operate a fixed cut-off date (FCOD) policy for animal testing. This means that after a certain date they don't conduct any animal tests, and have a policy of not using any ingredients tested on animals by their suppliers from a fixed date.

The *FCOD* is the most widely accepted non-animal testing policy and the most reliable.

"This product is not tested on animals" or "is cruelty free."
Some products may not carry these logos and still say they are "not tested on animals." However, this may mean that the final product has not been tested on animals, but the ingredients are. Or, that the suppliers of their ingredients do test them on animals.

If you are unsure, always ask before you buy. You have every right to be fully informed. But, if in doubt, don't buy. Sadly not all shop assistants are well informed.

TIP
Not all of the companies who would qualify for the Leaping Bunny logo or to get some form of cruelty free accreditation, apply. You may have to do your own research before you buy.

Why is the Leaping Bunny trademark the best?
The Leaping Bunny logo, which is used throughout the world, currently is the only one that guarantees a final product and the ingredients it contains have not been tested by that company on animals and that the ingredients have not been tested on animals by their suppliers. Other companies may have a similar logo on their products, including that of a rabbit (as there is no copyright on that), but that can be very misleading and does not guarantee they are cruelty free.

Example – Say a company called All Creatures, don't test their products or ingredients on animals, but they do buy, use and benefit financially from chemical ingredients that have recently been tested on animals by their suppliers. They would quite rightly not be on the list of companies that qualify for the Humane Cosmetic Standard and Humane Household Standard, which allows them to use the Leaping Bunny trademark (these qualifying companies must allow various checks to be made).

Companies who do qualify don't conduct animal testing or use ingredients from companies that do animal testing and must show that this has been the case for five years (that's what's known as a 'fixed cut off date). Therefore, our made up company wouldn't qualify.

Note – other cruelty free lists may be less strict than the Leaping Bunny one.

Other rabbit & no animal testing logos
Products may often carry a rabbit or similar cruelty free logo, making you think they are cruelty free, but this may not be the case.

Or, they may say one of the following -

"This product contains no animal ingredients." - Reading this you may be misled into thinking this product is cruelty free, but this simply means what it says and does not tell you anything about whether it's tested on animals. Just because a product is not tested on animals does not mean it contains no animal ingredients.

"Neither this product or its ingredients are tested on animals." - This appears on products that often feature a rabbit type logo that's not the same as the Leaping Bunny version. It may be these items genuinely are cruelty free and that the company either doesn't want to carry the guaranteed cruelty free logo, or hasn't yet qualified for it as they need to prove that for five years they haven't tested the finished products or the ingredients on animals and that their suppliers haven't either. Or, perhaps they are simply unaware that they can apply.

"This product is not tested on animals." - This says nothing about whether the ingredients were tested on animals.

How do I check if a company or its products are cruelty free? Do they have Leaping Bunny logo on their products? If you don't find one ,then the chances are they are not cruelty free. Either, consult the lists on the Leaping Bunny (www.leapingbunny.org) or go cruelty free sites (www.gocrueltyfree.org) - they have lists of companies worldwide who don't test on animals, or contact the company direct and ask just what their policy is on animal testing. The more people who do that the more likely companies will get the message that consumers want cruelty free cosmetics.

The Australian site www.choosecrueltyfree.org.au is the number one site for Australians who want to go cruelty free.

TIP
Big companies may claim to be "against animal testing," on their websites and leaflets, but unless they are on a reliable cruelty free list or carry a Leaping Bunny logo on their products, there's a good chance they use animal testing.

"Whenever people say, "We mustn't be sentimental," you can take it they are about to do something cruel. And if they add, "We must be realistic,' they mean they are going to make money out of it."
Brigid Brophy, English-Irish novelist and playwright

Myths about cruelty free cosmetics

To justify testing cosmetics on animals, companies may come up with seemingly good reasons why they do test on animals. But these are generally myths.

1. Without animal testing products can't be safe.
Not testing on animals doesn't mean no testing at all. In fact, it may mean more reliable testing, because instead of animals, human skin grown in test tubes may be used instead. Skin patch tests on humans who can tell the testers how they are feeling, unlike animals who have to suffer in silence, can also be used.

Researchers can also tell whether products will be safe by using ingredients already known to be safe.

2. No animal testing means less effective products.
Not so. I use Superdrug's own brand cosmetics. They are all carry the leaping bunny logo and are cruelty free. Most are vegan as well as vegetarian. There are many more companies that are cruelty free, but remember, things can change at any time, so always look for that white bunny on the label.

3. The law requires animal testing.
No, it doesn't. In the US, Neither the U.S. Food and Drug Administration (FDA) nor the U.S. Consumer Product Safety Commission require animal testing for cosmetics or household products. There is enough existing information to make testing for products obsolete.

FACT
In Canada, there is a legal requirement to test medicines on animals, but not cosmetics.

FACT
When companies tell you they must carry out animal testing by law, it's a lie. They may be using new ingredients, which under the law need to have been tested before they go on sale, but this does not have to be on animals.

Cell cultures could be used, or human skin generated in a test tube, or even human volunteers.

MYTH
All products carrying the bunny logo are suitable for vegetarians and vegans
This is a very common misconception. The Leaping Bunny certification is a guarantee of no animal testing, not of no animal products having been used like gelatine (it comes from the inside of animals' skin and bones), animal glycerin (made from animal fats, collagen (usually from fish, although you can get synthetic collagen) and tallow (from bones), and cochineal (crushed insects who produce a reddish/pinkish color found in cosmetics).

To ensure products are suitable for vegetarians or vegans and that they don't contain any animal products like fish oil, check the labeling for the V for vegetarian symbol or vegan logo. There are different variations of the suitable for vegans logo, but generally they have the word vegan included. The Superdrug products I mentioned, have the BUAV version of the leaping bunny logo and suitable for vegetarians and vegans on the label.

TIP
In the case of vegetarian, they may have just a simple V or a V sign with the wording Vegetarian Society approved written above it. The Vegetarian Society is the most reliable of all vegetarian logos as products that carry the logo (food, household products, confectionary and cosmetics) are scrupulously checked.

TIP
If suitable for vegans, they may carry an approved by the Vegan Society logo. You can search for vegetarian and vegan products at the www.gocrueltyfree.org site by selecting the Vegan/Vegetarian Society Approved options as you search.

Note – The reverse is also true. Just because a product has the appropriate vegan or vegetarian symbol does not mean it's not tested on animals.

"Beauty begot of the ugliness of animal testing is not true beauty; it's ugliness."
Anon

Cruelty Free cleaning and household products

It's not only food and cosmetics that can involve cruelty animal testing. Many things we use everyday like washing powder, air fresheners, window and toilet cleaners, furniture polish are usually tested on animals: both the ingredients and the finished product.

If you want to avoid buying household products, including cleaners and toiletries that are tested on animals, then there is a site that lists cruelty free companies at
www.gocrueltyfree.org

You can search by country including the USA, Canada, Australia, the UK, Singapore, Ireland, India and South Africa. In some countries, brands are only available online.
You can also search by either cosmetics or household products.

FACT
In the UK in 2008, *the BUAV* (the British Union for Abolition of Vivisection) launched a campaign to end the use of animals in the testing of household products. Their campaign is fittingly called **Clean Up Cruelty**. The campaign has gained support from politicians, retailers and the public.

FACT
In the UK, certified cruelty free household products and cleaners (they carry *the BUAV* Leaping Bunny logo) are made by stores such as *the Co-op*, *Marks and Spencer*. Other top brands include *Astonish*, *Method* and *Faith In Nature*.

FACT
In 2011, **Superdrug** were given the Leaping Bunny accreditation to put on their household products, showing they hadn't been tested on animals. They also have a very popular cosmetics brand that carries the logo.

You can check it out on their website
http://www.superdrug.com/brandshop/B

Animal testing facts in a nutshell

1. The animal testing of cosmetics is not a legal requirement in America, Canada, Australia or the UK.

2. By law, all cosmetics and that includes toiletries must be tested on animals in China for them to be sold in China.

3. Animals suffer badly during tests and the results are often unreliable.

4. A number of non-animal tests are now in use and more are being developed as you read this.

5. The leaping bunny symbol is used worldwide and shows that a product has not been tested on animals and neither have its ingredients. This also includes them having the final product or ingredients tested on animals by others on their behalf.

6. If a product doesn't carry the international renowned leaping bunny logo, then it's probably tested on animals.

7. Companies who benefit from animal testing will not get the Leaping Bunny accreditation symbol if they apply.

8. If you want to know if a product is tested on animals, write to the company and ask what their policy is.

9. Many companies beat the cosmetics animal testing ban in their country by conducting animal testing outside their own country.

"Slavery can only be abolished by raising the character of the people who compose the nation; and that can be done only by showing them a higher one."
Maria W Chapman, slavery abolitionists.

Chapter 7
Shop Kind

These days more and more people want to be ethical shoppers because they want to know that the things they buy were produced by workers who were paid a fair price for their wares.

This chapter is devoted to ethical shopping and the various schemes to ensure producers of goods get treated fairly, because being cruelty free means not being cruel to our fellow human beings too.

What is an ethical shopper?
Normally, ethical shoppers want to know if –
1. Products are tested on animals

2. Products were produced using slave labor or child labor

3. Products were made by workers who were paid a fair wage

4. Products were made by workers who had decent working conditions i.e. they weren't over-worked or made to work in a factory without proper ventilation

5. Products were made from sustainable materials that are not going to run out and cause environmental problems such as pollution and damage to the o-zone level.

6. Where relevant if products are made from recycled materials and the packaging can be recycled. That way the packaging doesn't end up in a landfill site.

.

How to become an ethical shopper

Being an ethical shopper isn't always easy. Often it isn't until you read about a company using slave labor and child labor that you become aware of the fact they have questionable ethics.

There is one way to guarantee that goods are ethical and that is by buying Fair Trade certified products (called just Fairtrade in the UK).

The UK's leading alternative consumer organization has a website at www.ethicalconsumer.org where brands are awarded points according on five different criteria:

1. environment (does the production of this product result in damage to the environment)
2. animals (was the product tested on animals, a product of factory farming and was animal welfare taken into account)

3. people (human and workers rights, irresponsible marketing and does the company profit from the arms trade)

4. politics (have there been calls to boycott the country's products, does the company use genetic engineering etc...)

5. product sustainability (is the product Fairtrade, organic, was animal welfare and the environment taken into account)

Note – Although this is a UK-based site, the information applies to many global brands that you can buy elsewhere in the world like America, Canada and South Africa.

Modern-day slavery

Slavery is meant to have been abolished, yet millions of workers throughout the world wouldn't know it. Under paid and over-worked, forced to work and live in conditions people in the West would consider shocking, slave laborers are living the modern-day equivalent of slavery.

FACT

Slave labor can happen anywhere. In 2011, it emerged that a 38-year-old Filipino woman was kept as a domestic slave by a Vancouver couple who brought her over from Hong Kong. They forced her to work all the time and emotionally and physically abused her. There have been several similar cases in the UK and the USA. Unscrupulous employees often stop people from leaving by hiding their passports or threatening to report them to the authorities.

FACT

In Dubai, in the United Arab Emirates, most of the luxury accommodation built was the work of hundreds of thousands of Asian workers who are paid low salaries and forced to exist in squalor. Many of them come from places like India where they have fled poverty. Many were recruited by unscrupulous recruitment firms who charged them hefty fees to come to the country.
Source – *Human Rights Watch.*

FACT

In 2007, *Topshop*, one of the leading fashion chains in the UK, was accused of underpaying Asian workers. They were reportedly paid what should be at least an hourly wage for working twelve-hour days. The owner of *Topshop*, Sir Philip Green said he was taking the allegations seriously and would be investigating.
Source – *The Sunday Times.*

Here are some more sobering statistics:

According to Anti-slavery International, millions of men, women and children throughout the world are forced to live as slaves. We may not think of these people as slaves, but that's exactly what they are. Exploited by being forced to work for little pay, they are often sold as though they are objects and not people. This is often done by traffickers who force people to work as some form of repayment for getting them into another country. This is called forced labor and is a form of slave labor.

According to *the International Labour Organization* (ILO) estimates, there are at least 12.3 million people in forced labor worldwide. A staggering 40-50 percent of them are children.

Figures from the US State Department claimed that an estimated 17,500 people are trafficked into the country every year, but this is only an estimate as the true figure is not known. Many of them are used as forced labor.

In 2009, budget high street chain *Primark* in the UK was accused of using slave labor. In a joint operation with the BBC, illegal immigrants were found to be working in sweatshops in Manchester for half the minimum wage payable by law.

TIP

Ask yourself if a garment you are buying seems too cheap. If it is the chances are it was made with slave labor. This keeps the store's costs down and allows them to sell cheap clothes.

"The world is indebted for all triumphs which have been gained by reason and humanity over error and oppression."
Thomas Jefferson, former US President.

What's a sweatshop?

The term was first heard in 1892 in reference to clothes makers in the USA and the atrocious working conditions they endured.

It's estimated that millions of people throughout the world work in poor, often unsanitary conditions, for long hours and very low pay. The problem is made worse by the practice of large companies contracting out work to countries that have poor labor laws. That way their labor costs will be low and their profit margins high.

These days although the conditions may have improved, sweatshops are guilty of labor violations. Things like using child labor and forcing workers to work on long after they should be allowed to go home and often for no extra pay just to meet targets. Note – in many cases sweatshop employers provide accommodation for their employees that is well below what we could consider a habitable standard (many people forced to share a single room, no toilet facilities or access to water for washing etc...) and they deduct the rent from their pitiful wages.

Sadly, sweatshops are mot just a problem in developing nations like India, there have also been instances of sweatshops in the USA, UK and Canada in what could rightly be termed modern day slavery.

Sweatshops in the West tend to employ vulnerable people who have no choice to work for them. People like single mothers, asylum seekers and those in the country illegally.

What's Fair Trade?

Fair Trade is the perfect name for it because the scheme means exactly what it says, namely that a fair trade is made.

This means:
1. The farmers are paid a fair price
2. The workers are paid a fair price

Fairtrade first appeared in the 1980's when coffee produced in Mexico was given the Fairtrade label and sold in Dutch supermarkets

By the late 80's and early 90's, the brand was sold in stores in the USA and Canada (under the Transfair label) and the UK (with the Fairtrade mark on the packaging), Japan and France amongst others.

TIP
The Fair Trade certification and *Fairtrade* labels now appear on a diverse variety of products like bananas, fruit juices, clothing, footballs, roses and chocolate.

What's the Fair Trade logo?
To make sure its Fair Trade, always look out for the distinctive label that says it's Fair Trade. In America, the label is a white square that says "Fair Trade USA" and then "every purchase matters."

In the UK, the Fairtrade label is a distinctive blue, green, white and black logo. When some people see it they say it looks a parrot or a leaf. The most popular interpretation is that the green represents grass, the blue the sky and the black dot and swirl a person with their hand raised aloft. It reads "Fairtrade Foundation" below the logo.

In Canada, the logo is the same as the UK logo except it reads Fairtrade at the bottom. There is also another logo that is a rectangle with Fair Trade certified at the top and certified equitable along the bottom. The logo for this one is a person (half white and half black) holding a bowl in either hand.

To learn more about Fair Trade certified products in the USA, visit http://fairtradeusa.org/
To learn more Fair Trade in Canada, go to http://fairtrade.ca
For the UK, go to www.fairtrade.org.uk
For South Africa, visit www.fairtrade.org.za
For Australia and New Zealand, visit www.fta.org.au

TIP
If you want to buy genuine Fairtrade products, they don't have to carry the label. You can buy it when you're on holiday simply by buying souvenirs from local people in street markets instead of in shopping complexes or in hotel shops.

FACT
A product carrying the Fair Trade (Fairtrade logo) doesn't mean that the company who produced it didn't use slave labor or child labor to make their other products. It refers to that product only.

FACT
In 2003, Fair Trade oranges from South Africa were put on the market.

FACT
The fastest growth in Fair Trade products, has been in coffee beans and in cocoa beans. This is because of the boom in coffee and chocolate sales.

FACT
In 2010, the first Fair Labor certified clothing arrived in the USA. For the first time Americans could identify clothes that guaranteed fair prices for the cotton producers and the clothes makers.

How do Fair Trade/Fairtrade ensure workers are treated fairly?

Producers are inspected by an organization called FLO-CERT who check to make sure that producers are contributing to the social and economic development of people through people's purchases. They are an independent company who offer Fairtrade certification to clients in more than 70 countries. To learn more about them visit www.flo-cert.net and click on "English."

Where can I buy Fair Trade/Fairtrade?

Most supermarket chains will sell at least some products carrying the certification even if it's only chocolate, coffee or bananas.

Big name brands that sell Fair Trade products include *Starbucks*, *Ben & Jerry's* and *Divine Chocolate*.

The UK is one of the largest markets for Fairtrade products. Most stores like *Marks and Spencer*, *Asda* and *the Co-Op* will sell Fairtrade coffee, chocolate and bananas.

There are lists also of stockists on the Fairtrade websites.

Is Fairtrade expensive?

Yes, it can be when compared to other products, but ask yourself this: is knowing that the workers who toiled to produce what you bought were paid fairly not worth the extra cost?

Why is the Fair Trade/Fairtrade label needed?

1. All over the world, farmers and workers are being exploited in some of the poorest countries.

2. Fair Trade raises the standard of living of workers throughout the world.

3. Fair Trade raises the salaries of workers so they can afford to feed their families.

4. Fair Trade prevents people in countries from being paid too little for the things they produce. In many countries people starve not because they don't produce anything to sell, but because they aren't paid a fair price for what they do produce.

5. Fair Trade helps improve people's working conditions.

6. Because consumers genuinely want to know that workers weren't exploited.

Child labor
Another reason why Fair Trade is needed, is to prevent the use of child labor.

According to the organization, *Stop Child Labor*, there are 218million child laborers in the world.

That's 218 million children who won't get to go to school.

218 million children, who are being exploited and who don't get to live a normal life. And that's just an estimate. The number may be much higher.

How can you know something was produced by child labor? Unfortunately, you can't tell whether child labor was used just by looking at the product. If it carries the Fair Trade label child labor will probably not have been used as the reason children are used is to provide cheap labor. Gaining the Fair Trade certification guarantees that farmers and workers are paid fairly.

If you're worried that child labor may have been used ask the store. They may not know or might not tell you the truth, but you have a right to ask. Every consumer has a right to know what they are buying.

How can I make sure the company I buy from doesn't exploit slave labor or children when they don't have the Fair Trade certification?
*Ask the company if they belong to the ETI (Ethical Trading Initiative). Member companies unite with volunteer organizations and trade unions and work towards improving the lives of workers Read more about it here www.ethicaltrade.org

*Ask what steps they have taken to ensure that their goods are not made by people who are underpaid and forced to work in poor conditions or by child labor. For instance, do they monitor the factories and the conditions that people work in? This is important because too often companies may contract out to self-employed agents or contractors and not directly find manufacturers themselves. Yet every company has a responsibility to know the ins and outs of its supply chain. As a consumer, you are entitled to know where the goods you buy or about to buy come from.

*Ask what steps they have taken to ensure that the raw materials used in their products were ethically sourced. Was the cocoa used in their chocolate products or the cotton in their t-shirts farmed by workers paid a fair wage? Unfortunately, many companies don't always have this information although their suppliers will.

*Ask if they paid a fair price for the goods. When companies don't and drive the prices down it's usually the workers who suffer by being asked to work more and longer for less in worse conditions.

*Carpets and rugs carrying the *GoodWeave* certification label and logo weren't made using illegal child labor. The mark used to be Rugmark but this changed in 2009. Read more about it the international scheme here
www.goodweave.org.uk/about-goodweave/about-goodweave.shtml
They also have a list of retailers on their website.

TIP
You will probably need to write to head office to get information on a company's animal testing policy, as staff might not be informed. If you don't get a reply that tells you what you want to know, then you can assume this company either isn't an ethical one or doesn't care enough to reply to potential customers.

TIP
Rather than buy from chain stores, why not buy from the people who make and sell their own wares like jewelry and t-shirts in malls and markets? That way you know the right people are making money.

Trafficked people
Slave labor doesn't always mean groups of people being forced to work for low wages in their own countries. It can also mean vulnerable people being brought or coming voluntarily to countries where we think there's no slavery. Many of these people are women and girls forced into the sex trade once they arrive (many are smuggled into the country) and they are what we would call trafficked. This is a very complex topic that would take a book of its own to cover.

If you live in the USA, report suspected trafficking to *the Department of Health and Human Services* (they have a 24hr hotline) and *the Department of Justice* sponsored **Trafficking in Persons** and **Worker Exploitation Task Force Complaint Line** (a toll free 24hr hotline).

For more details of human trafficking in the USA and non-governmental organizations you can contact, advice and contact details, go to www.humantrafficking.org

In some cases, the victims of trafficking may be given permanent immigration status.

In the UK, Canada and Australia contact the police.

Domestic slaves
Other people may be enticed to come and live in countries like the USA, Canada and the UK with the promise of a good job and salary. Once they arrive, they discover that rather than earn good money as an au pair, nanny or housekeeper, they have to live in people's homes and are treated like domestic slaves. They may also be subjected to physical and mental abuse on a regular basis.

Generally, these people have come of their own free will and are not trafficked, but once they arrive and find out they've been lied to about the kind of life they will lead, it's too late to leave. They may be prevented from leaving by their employer taking their passport or not paying them the salary they've worked for.

Employers may also use the threat of contacting immigration and having them deported; something, which would terrify anyone who's living in a strange country, even if they do have a visa. They may also lie about their employee stealing from them to frighten them into staying.

How to spot a domestic slave

Are they allowed to leave their work site alone to do things like go and buy groceries, or are they always accompanied by someone from the household?

*Do they ever get a day off? Most employees should get at least one day off a week.

*Have you ever seen them out on their own? Say at a movie or out shopping.

*Do they look like they are living in fear? Are they nervous?

*Have they been threatened by anyone in the household?

*Have you seen any evidence that they've been assaulted? Bruises, cuts, broken bones, torn clothes?

*Are they shabbily dressed/ always wearing the same clothes? This is a sign they are not being paid a decent salary or even any salary at all. Often employers make "deductions" from their salaries for breakages, food and board when they have no right to do that.

*Do they have a contract of employment that details their terms and conditions? Are they paid the minimum wage or much less?

*Are they ever allowed to use the phone and when they do is someone always listening in?

*Do they ever get any mail? If they don't this might be a sign that they are not allowed to contact anyone.

FACT

The majority of cases of domestic slavery in the USA are never prosecuted. The victims are too scared; they can't speak the language and are ashamed of what's happened to them.

FACT

In 2010, over 15,000 domestic workers were brought to the UK. Charities claim that many end up as slaves working for rich families. Many domestic workers are paid a pittance, whilst others may have their salaries withheld for no good reason. Their passports may also be confiscated by their employers to prevent them from leaving.

What you can do to help

If you suspect that someone is being kept as a domestic slave, there are things you can do:

1. If you believe someone is a domestic slave, try to talk to them and tell them that they have rights. For instance, their employer has no right to take away their passport. They also have a right to be paid a decent wage.

2. Ask them to write down everything that happens to them in their employer's house, such as details of how long they work and any abuse they are subjected to, both mental and physical.

3. If you hear them being physical harmed or see any evidence that they have been assaulted, call the police immediately.

4. Get numbers for women's shelters (refuges) as most domestic slaves are female. The most important thing is to get them out of the situation. If you live in the UK, contact your local citizen's advice bureau for details.

5. If their employer is withholding the person's passport or visa to prevent them from leaving, get the police involved. Often a visit from the police will make employers hand over passports that they have no right to have in the first place.

TIP
If you live in the USA, contact *The American Civil Liberties Union* (ACLU) for advice. They have affiliates in every US state and Puerto Rico and can offer legal advice. Go to www.aclu.org/affiliates for details.

TIP
If you live in the UK, there is a charity called Kalayaan who help migrant domestic workers. See www.kalayaan.org.uk for details.

TIP
Domestic workers who believe they are being mistreated, can also contact the Employment Standards Information Centre.

"Progress is impossible without change; and those who cannot change their minds, cannot change anything."
George Bernard Shaw.

Chapter 8
25 Ways to Create a More Compassionate World

Famine. War. Child abuse. Animal cruelty. It can be distressing seeing all the bad things that go on in the world and feeling a sense of hopelessness.

Where do you begin to make a difference? To change things and make it a better world for everyone?

The good news is that we can all live a more compassionate life with the choices we make. Whether it's donating money to charities that give people the means to feed themselves, deciding not to go on holiday to a region of Spain where they have still have bullfighting, or looking out for our elderly neighbors, we can all do something to create a better world for us all to live in. And, the good news is we can start today.

Here are some easy ways to live cruelty free and make the world we live in a better place -

1. Support World Vision's Micro scheme (or your country's version)

The charity **World Vision** run a micro-finance program where they offer loans to people in developing countries such as Rwanda, the Philippines, Cambodia and Armenia to set up in business. The money goes towards things like stock and land for people who want to set up a business, or need money to continue with an existing business. You decide which entrepreneur you wish to support (there are profiles of would be business people on the site along with a graph of how much money they need) and you donate however much you can afford.

You also get to track your chosen person's progress and so feel part of what they are doing.

To find out more, visit www.worldvisionmicro.org

Canada
They also have a similar scheme in Canada. The minimum donation is $5 Canadian Dollars. Visit **World Vision Canada** http://www.worldvision.ca/OURWORK/Economic%20Devel opment/Pages/EconomicDevelopment.aspx

FACT
Most of the businesses that get micro-finance, repay their loans and the money goes back into the scheme, so the money you pay in will keep on working, ensuring that people in poor countries can keep building a better life for themselves and their children.

FACT
All recipients of loans are vetted to guarantee they are legitimate and their progress followed.

2. Avoid buying cosmetics that contain cruelly obtained ingredients

In 2011, *Lush Cosmetics* launched a week long campaign at its stores in Hong Kong and Macau (like Hong Kong, its one of the regions governed by China) to highlight the plight of sharks. The reason a cosmetics company decided to take this action was because as well as being killed for their flesh (to go in shark fin soup) and cartilage (as an ingredient for health supplements like Chondroitin), sharks are also being killed for their oil that is used in creams and lotions and Omega 3 fish oil supplements. This shark liver oil contains **squalene** and Pristane, as well as Omega 3 fatty acids.

TIP
Shark liver oil can also be called Squalamine.

FACT
Sharks are killed by being harpooned and dragged through the water, whilst in agony. They suffocate when dragged out of the water.

FACT
Many of the sharks that are hunted for their oil are endangered species.

FACT
Even when sharks aren't been deliberately targeted, they're often trapped in nets, as are many different species die in these nets, including dolphins, porpoises, turtles, rays and whales also die in the nets.

FACT
In some countries like the USA, fishermen hunt sharks just to collect their jaws as souvenirs. Baby sharks are also killed.

TIP

There have been various medical claims about the powers of shark liver oil, including that it heals wounds and helps ease respiratory disorders, but none of these claims have been validated and physicians don't prescribe it. If you have medical problems, see a doctor.

FACT
No research has been done to determine whether shark liver oil interacts with other medications and stop them from working.

FACT
As a result of the demand for shark products, sharks are now an endangered species.

"How wonderful it is that nobody need wait a single moment before starting to improve the world."
Anne Frank

3. Avoid buying cheap clothing because it may come at a human cost
The explosion in cheap clothing may be good for consumers, but it's certainly not good for workers who make the garments and don't get a fair salary for doing it.

Everybody loves a bargain, but sometimes the reason stores can afford to sell things like clothing so cheaply is because the people who make those items are paid so little. This may not always be with the stores' knowledge as many of them rely on agencies to recruit workers mainly in countries like India and Malaysia, but they still have a duty to make sure their products are ethically sourced.

TIP

As much as possible, try and buy clothing that carries the Fair Trade certification logo, or says Fairtrade on it. That way you can ensure workers are not being taken advantage of.

If you are unable to do that, as in some countries Fair Trade clothing is difficult if not impossible to find, buy clothes that carry an ethical label or say they were made with Fairtrade/Fair Trade certified cotton.

Another good way to make sure whoever produced what you buy has made a fair wage from their work is to buy jewelry and clothes from trade fairs that people have made themselves.

FACT
Fair Trade clothing has arrived in the USA. To find out more about Transfer USA Fair Trade Certified label go to www.ecouterre.com/first-fair-trade-certified-clothing-arrives-in-the-us

TIP
There are online stores where you can buy Fair Trade clothing, such as www.fairindigo.com and www.anniegreenabelle.com a store that will ship throughout the USA and the UK.

You may also find www.sweatfree.org/shoppingguide useful as it offers a range of sweatshop free apparel

Canada
In Canada, it is possible to buy garments made of Fair Trade cotton. Look out for those labels. Find out more by going to http://fairtrade.ca/en/products/cotton

UK
If you live in the UK, you'll find a list of places where you can buy Fairtrade products. See
http://www.fairtrade.org.uk/en/buying-fairtrade

Australia
For more information on Fairtrade in Australia, visit www.fta.org.au
The main Fairtrade products on sale in Australia are bananas, coffee, tea, and chocolate, sports balls like footballs, cotton and nuts.

FACT
Fairtrade products are often better quality because they tend to use organic practices and not use insecticides and other chemicals.

FACT
If workers are paid fairly, then stores will charge a fair price for the goods.

4. Avoid circuses where wild animals are used
The life of a circus animal is often not a happy one. Many animals such as bears, lions, tigers and elephants originally came from the wild and are mistreated to get them to perform. Well, it's not natural for animals to balance things on their heads and ride on tricycles – not unless it's a cartoon.

To get them to perform for audiences, their so-called trainers tend to use two methods – punishment and deprivation. Animals are beaten if they won't perform and are starved. They might have tight collars put on them, be subjected to electric shocks and cattle prods, and be jabbed with metal hooks that tear through their skin.

Their sad plight doesn't end there. Circus animals are often kept in cramped cages without enough space and are not adequately exercised or fed. They may be forced to eat and sleep in the same cage where they do the toilet.

FACT
Circuses often get away with mistreating their animals because training sessions aren't monitored by animal welfare bodies. The only way people know what goes on, is because animal charities like *PETA* have recorded undercover footage.

FACT
Because of ill-treatment, there have been cases where elephants and other circus animals have gotten loose and fearing for public safety, they've been shot.

FACT
In the UK, British politicians voted to ban the use of wild animals in circuses. In some UK towns and cities circuses with wild animals were already banned.

FACT
Circuses can be entertaining without any animals being used. Think of the Big Top and you think of trapeze artists flying through the air and clowns soaking people with water hidden in their bowties.

> *"Service to others is the rent you pay for your room here on earth."*
> Muhammad Ali

5. Don't vacation or buy properties in countries where there are human rights abuses like Saudi Arabia.

Did you know that there is a country where women are not allowed to drive, or go places without a male chaperone (who must be a family member) and if they do they can be thrown in prison? Where punishments for theft can mean limbs being amputated? And, if you're considered to be a "sexual deviant," which can mean anything from being gay to sharing a room with a member of the opposite sex you're not married to, you can be flogged?

For all its glorious beaches and luxurious hotels, Saudi Arabia is a country accused of the worst kind of human rights abuses by Amnesty International and Human Rights Watch. The country doesn't have a democracy; what it does have is a ruling royal family.

Women are not treated as equals to men. They're not allowed to vote. A guardian system is also in place whereby women are not allowed to do things we all take for granted like accepting employment, getting married, buying or selling a house, studying or even traveling without the permission of a male guardian who can be a father, husband or brother.

Despite the country's human rights abuses, it's seen as a dream destination for a vacation and an ideal place to own a holiday property. Saudi Arabia isn't alone in not treating its citizens and immigrant workers fairly.

FACT
Dubai in the United Arab Emirates, is considered another dream vacation spot because of its beautiful beaches. The country's estimated 250,000 foreign laborers who built most of the properties wouldn't think so. According to Human Rights Watch, conditions they live in are described as "less than human."

FACT

It was being ostracized from the international community and not being allowed to take part in sporting events that led to the end of apartheid in South Africa: a system whereby people were separated by race with the black majority kept in poverty. You see, people power can make a difference.

6. Don't go to the dogs (watch or bet on dog racing)

It's estimated that in the UK, tens of thousands of greyhounds are killed each year for no other reason than they can't race any more or they weren't quite fast enough. The average age that greyhounds retire at is less than three years old as this is when they start to lose their speed. As a result of this, many greyhounds end up in need of new homes if they're not euthanized (killed).

The risk of injuries to racing dogs is very high. Many dogs end up crippled. Race fixing and dog doping also goes on and there have been cases of dogs being given cocaine.

There have been incidences in the UK where dogs that don't make it as racing dogs have been killed. In 2006, The Sunday Times newspaper in the UK, filmed two greyhound trainers taking two of their dogs who'd "underperformed" to be shot dead by David Smith, who was dubbed the "unofficial executioner" in the industry. The dog killer is said to have killed 10,000 greyhounds in 15 years. Both dogs were less than three-years-old and the trainers allegedly had them killed because a greyhound charity didn't have the space to take them for a week.

A court fined Smith who used a bolt gun to kill the dogs, £2,000 not for killing the dogs as he broke no animal welfare laws, but because he didn't have a permit to bury them on his land. He left Durham Crown Court to a chorus of "murderer" after being described as "the greyhound serial killer."

Greyhound trainers having their retired dogs killed; is commonplace. Others dogs end up being taking in by charities. The majority of greyhounds were deliberately bred for racing.

FACT
Live greyhound racing is banned in a number of American states. There are also a number of states where no racing takes place because there isn't the demand or desire for it.

TIP
Throughout the USA, Canada and Europe (including the UK) there are retired greyhounds needing good homes. Go to www.adopt-a-greyhound.org/directory/list.cfm for a list. You can select by country.

The Retired Greyhound Trust in the UK, are constantly on the look out for homes for unwanted dogs. Visit www.retiredgreyhounds.co.uk for details.

FACT
Greyhounds make perfect family pets: they're laid back, gentle and good with children. They will chase cats though.

"Cruelty is one fashion statement we can all do without."
Rue McClanahan

7. Write a letter for Amnesty International

The whole reason that Amnesty International came into being was to protect and defend human rights throughout the world. One of the ways they do this is by getting people like you to write letters to politicians on behalf of victims of human rights abuses. Many of these victims are political prisoners who are locked away in conditions that many of us would find barbaric and some are tortured.

This is often for no other reason than they disagree with the government of the time, usually because of how they treat people.

The organization has a global presence and has many different campaigns running at one time.

For more details, visit the relevant site-
www.amnestyusa.org
www.amnesty.ca
www.amnesty.org/en/region/south-africa
http://amnesty.org.uk
www.amnesty.org.au

FACT
For many prisoners, getting a letter is the only contact they have with the outside world. It lets them know that they haven't been abandoned.

TIP
Avoid discussing politics and instead concentrate on things like what your daily life is like. Avoid depressing subjects to.

8. Buy products from cruelty free fashion designers.
Stella McCartney is famous for her no fur and no leather stance in her designs, whilst companies like Calvin Klein and Herve Leger have strict no fur policies.

The reverse also applies: don't buy from designers who favor fur like *Burberry*, *Fendi*, *Gucci* and *Pucci*.

Note – leather isn't considered cruelty free. This is because the animals it comes from (usually cows) are killed and usually come from factory farms. This makes leather similar to fur in that the animals are killed to produce it.

TIP
If you decide to boycott any companies because of their pro-fur stance, write to them and tell them why you are not buying their product.

It's not just fur that you need to look out for if you want to buy cruelty free fashion –

1. For anyone who loves horses, the prospect of ponies being sent to the slaughterhouse where they are killed and then skinned, will seem repugnant. Yet this does happen. Pony leather is used in handbags, shoes and purses.

2. Kangaroo leather – after hearing how kangaroos were slaughtered to make soccer (football) boots, David Beckham switched to boots made from synthetic materials instead.

3. Snakes and lizards are also killed so their skin can be turned into shoes, handbags and belts.

4. Seal skin is a kind of fur and may be used for outer garments like coats, gloves and mufflers.

5. Alligators, which should be in the wild, are farmed so they can be killed for their skin.

6. Leather isn't always a slaughterhouse byproduct from cows. There have been cases where cat and dog skin has been found in leather. This is believed to have come from animals slaughtered in China.

TIP
Fur favoring companies change all the time, so it's always best to check.

FACT
Instead of buying *Ugg* boots, Pamela Anderson who famously wore them with her red swimsuit on Baywatch before she knew they were made out of sheepskin, suggests you buy *Stella McCartney* or *Juicy Boots* instead.

FACT
Leather is never labeled with animal of origin, so you never know what animal it came from and how they were treated.

FACT
It takes fifteen times the amount of energy to make one real fur coat as it does to make a fake one.

FACT
Faux or fake fur and leather can look as good as the real thing, but it's cheaper to buy and cruelty free.

FACT
The sale of sealskin is banned throughout the European Union. In Canada and America seal fur is still on sale.

"Wherever a man turns he can find someone who needs him."
Albert Schweitzer

9. Look out for your neighbors.

We've all read stories about people who have passed away in their own homes and their bodies have been left undiscovered until someone complained about the smell. We've all shook our heads and thought how terrible that was. But, how many of us have decided that from now on we'll check up our neighbors to make sure they're doing okay and don't need help with something like getting groceries in and walking the dog?

Loneliness is one of the cruelest things there is. Does it really take up too much of our time to say hello and to ask our neighbors how they are doing?

TIP
The next time you cook or bake something and have some to spare, why not go round to your neighbor's. It's the neighborly thing to do. Or take in their mail when they are out. Small gestures like this help build relationships.

Other times to see if your neighbor is all right –
1. Has the power or water gone off? Check that your neighbor is okay.

2. Is it particularly cold or warm? If your neighbor has health problems, is elderly or disabled, maybe you should go check on them?

3. Have you not seen them for a while? Drop by.

4. You don't see any lights on at night. Could they have fallen?

5. There have been robberies in the area. Maybe they need your help to make them home more secure by installing new locks or just need some reassurance that you will keep an eye on their home and look out for anything suspicious.

TIP

Why not start a neighborhood watch? All the neighbors could get together say once every two weeks for drinks and nibbles and discuss any concerns they have. You could take it in turns to host the meeting.

TIP

Have a street party. Perfect for getting to know the neighbors.

10. Don't do shark cage diving/baiting.

This is where you go inside a shark proof cage and are lowered into the water. You may throw in food to get the sharks to come to you. Although the sharks are not harmed in any way, marine biologists believe that this new craze causes sharks to see human beings as food because they become acquainted with the scent. Sharks are then killed when they attack or there seems a threat of them attacking.

Think of it a bit like this. There's a lion in a cage and humans are dangled in front of that lion. There's no chance of the lion getting the people, but then one day the lion escapes and because it was tantalized by the smell of humans it goes and eats one. The lions end up being killed for just doing what comes naturally.

FACT

There has been an increase in shark attacks. Animal behaviorists believe this is linked to the popularity of shark cage diving.

FACT
Shark cages are a popular tourist attraction in countries like South Africa. In that country there is an organization called Surfers Against Shark Diving in South Africa. They believe that the rise in the number of attacks on humans is down to shark cage diving and the practice of chumming, which involves using a combination of blood, fish and meat to encourage and entice the sharks to get close enough to the boats for the people in cages to see and take pictures. See www.stopsharkcagediving.com for more information.

11. Donate your old spectacles to charity.
Can you think what it would be like to be unable to see? Some charities have a scheme whereby you donate your old glasses or spectacles and they are given to someone less fortunate so they can see. Many recipients are in the Third World.

As well as raising money to buy prescription glasses for people who can't afford them in the USA, **New Eyes for the Needy** also give donated glasses to people in need abroad. Movie star Jake Gyllenhaal is a supporter of the organization that has helped over 7million people to see again.

Visit www.neweyesfortheneedy.org for details, including of how to ship your glasses. They also accept hearing aids, jewelry and giftware to raise funds.

TIP
The Lions Club International have *Lions Eyeglass Recycling Centers* (LERCs) located around the world - the USA, Australia, Canada, France, Italy, South Africa and Spain. Glasses collected are then sorted through by volunteers. Find out more at their site www.lionsclubs.org/EN/our-work/sight-programs/eyeglass-recycling/lions-eyeglass-recycling-centers.php

TIP

If you live in the UK, you can donate your glasses by taking them to any opticians. You can find the guidelines here http://www.visionaidoverseas.org/resources/49/how-to-get-recycled-spectacles-to-vision-aid-overseas-via-dx

TIP

Don't send cases for glasses or spectacle cases as these are not needed. Opticians will know how to pack spectacles so they won't be damaged.

12. Don't buy puppies from puppy mills (also called puppy farms)

To feed the huge demand for puppies, more and more puppy mills are opening up. In these places, the mother dogs are usually kept in a confined space (usually a cage), in converted barns or sheds, often for 24-hours a day, with no access to the outdoors.

They have one litter of puppies and are then bred again and again until they are too old to have any puppies.

In a nutshell, puppy mills are the factory farming of dogs. As with factory farming of cattle, little attention is paid to the welfare of the dogs. The most important thing to the owners of these places is making as much money as possible from as little outlay as possible. This means making as many puppies as possible even if it's detrimental to the welfare of the mother dogs.

FACT

Where I live, a few people have adopted dogs rescued from puppy mills. At the start, the dogs had little hair, were sickly because their bodies had been leached of vitamins and they'd been kept in squalor, and they were terrified of others dogs and people. This is the reality of puppy farms.

•

There are a number of reasons why you should never buy a puppy from a puppy farm –

1. Mother dogs are simply there to have as many litters of pups as possible. As soon as they've had a litter they are bred again. Many end up being killed when they become too tired or old to breed and outlive their usefulness.

2. During their horrendous lives, mother dogs may never see daylight and may have to lie on the same bedding they have to do the toilet on because they are never allowed to go outside. The reason they are not allowed out, is because it means less work for the people who are employed by these farms. Employees tend to be untrained and poorly paid.

3. Often minimum welfare standards are not even met for the mother dogs and their puppies. The mothers can become ill and so can their puppies through lack of proper nutrition, sunlight and infections caused by dirty environments.

4. It's more likely that a puppy bought from a puppy mill will be sickly or even have to be put down than a puppy bought from a breeder who breeds dogs in their own homes. It's very common for the owners of these places to be sued when people take home their puppies and discover they have illnesses caused by inbreeding, poor hygiene standards and poor nutrition.

5. Puppy mills puppies often have behavioral problems because they have not been properly socialized. This means they can be very aggressive or go the other way and be timid to the point where they are scared of everything including people.

How to avoid buying from puppy mills

Despite the shocking stories, many people still continue to give money to puppy mills without even realizing it.

Here are some tips to help you avoid unwittingly buying a puppy from a puppy mill or puppy farm –

*Think of adopting instead. Rescue centers and shelters have dogs of all ages.

*Always ask to see the puppy in its home environment and never agree to meet anyone who is selling a puppy in a public place like a car park.

*Ask the breeder questions and ask to visit. Any reputable breeder will expect this. It's the ones who seem tight-lipped or reluctant for you to visit who might be the ones with puppy mills.

*Make sure you see the puppy with the rest of the litter and if possible see the father. Does the puppy look lively and healthy?

*Puppies should always come with paperwork. This should show whether they have been vaccinated and have been to see a vet. Many breeders make sure puppies are vaccinated before they are found new homes. They should also have been wormed as all puppies are born with worms. This is natural.

*Get a dog by word of mouth from someone you know well and trust. Most puppies from puppy mills are advertised on the Internet and in local newspapers and shops windows. Buyers are unaware of where they come from.

*Never buy a dog from a pet shop. There is a good chance the ones they sell come from puppy mills. Some pet super stores may also sell puppies from puppy mills.

*If the seller wants to sell you the puppy before its eight weeks old, you should be concerned. Puppies should stay with their mothers until they are at least eight weeks old. This is to ensure they get enough nutrients from their mother's milk.

*Try and see your puppy on at least two different visits before you take him home. Responsible breeders won't mind if you do this.

FACT
Since the 1980s, The Humane Society of the United States has been fighting to shut down puppy mills as they believe they are cruel and inhumane.

FACT
Most of the puppy mills, are in the UK are in Wales and Ireland. In Ireland, puppy farms are not regulated.

FACT
The conditions in some puppy mills are so bad that if you kept your pet dog in those conditions you would probably be prosecuted for animal cruelty.

TIP
Why not adopt a dog or cat from a shelter or rescue centre? All over the world, dogs are put down for no other reason than they don't have a home. This problem is made worse by the demand for puppies, usually pedigree ones, many of whom end up in animal shelters and with charities as unwanted pets. Wherever you live, there will be an animal shelter near you. If you don't feel you can see all the dogs needing homes, ask the staff to choose one for you. They will do this by asking you questions such as if you have children, a garden and whether you are at home all day.

TIP

Because of too much inbreeding, many pedigree dogs are born with health conditions they would not otherwise have like epilepsy and hip dysphasia. People buying pedigree dogs, adds to this problem because more dogs with these problems are brought into the world to be sold in order to meet the demand. Often pedigree dogs end up in shelters because their owners can't afford the vet bills to treat conditions caused by bad breeding.

TIP

There are also dogs that need to be fostered. This is where people are needed to temporarily look after a dog when their owner for some reason can't look after them for a period of time, say they are in hospital or moving into accommodation for a short period of time that doesn't allow pets.

Animal charities may also need foster carers for animals that need to finish a course of medical treatment before they are fostered.

TIP

Animal shelters also need dog walkers and people to clean out kennels. Why not volunteer?

"Charity sees the need, not the cause."
German Proverb

13. Teach adults how to read and write

What could exclude people from society more than them not being able to read or write? Literacy problems can stop you from doing a lot of things like getting a job (how can you fill in the application form, far less write a CV), enjoying a good book and even going shopping (reading packaging would be impossible).

The good news is that there are adult literacy classes that can help and you could be making a real difference by volunteering to be a tutor.

In the USA, in order to get citizenship, applicants have to pass a simple reading and writing exam as well as learn about American history and culture. Many of these people go to literacy and citizenship classes to learn and these classes need volunteers to help students. Ask your local college or search www.literacydirectory.org for details of adult literacy classes near you, then contact the learning institutions and ask if they need volunteers.

UK
In the UK, there are colleges and community learning centers offering classes to help people of all abilities to improve their reading and writing skills. These classes need volunteers to assist teachers. Qualifications aren't needed, but you may be given some training, which could even lead to a qualification. Some of the classes are aimed at people who have newly arrived in the country.

Australia
Asylum Seekers Centres need volunteer teachers. See www.refugeecouncil.org.au and click on get involved for more information on that and other possible volunteer opportunities.

Would you make a good teacher?

Before you volunteer, ask yourself –
1. Do you have patience and understanding needed to be a good teacher?

2. Are you a good listener?

3. Are your English skills good, or do you have problems with your spelling? If so, it might not be a good idea to become a teacher.

4. If the person you are helping can speak little English will you still be able to make yourself understood? This is the key to being a good teacher.

5. Can you get on well with people from all backgrounds and ages? You will be assigned pupils.

6. Do you think you could motivate someone to learn, including encourage them to persevere when things aren't going well?

7. Do you have the time to devote to helping someone? There's no point in you volunteering to help someone and then stopping classes because you have other commitments as often tutoring will be on a one on one basis.

TIP
Have you considered teaching English to those who speak another language? This can be extremely rewarding and the good news is that teachers are wanted all around the world. As well as helping people and earning some money, you may get the chance to travel. This is called Teaching English as a Foreign language, or TEFL, and you will need to undergo very detailed training first. You would have to pay for the training.

To read more about it, go to www.tefl.com
They have a list of available jobs throughout the world.

14. Don't attend or bet on the three-day English Grand National event.

●

Imagine a sporting event where participants die. Should it still go on? Would it still go on?

Between 1987 and 2011, 20 horses have died on the world famous Grand National course at Aintree in Liverpool in the UK. 9 of those deaths were in the big race and the other 11 were on shorter races that are run on the same course during the first two days of the three day race meeting.

There is no official record of the total number of horses that have died in the big race as it is not good for the horseracing community to advertise this. In fact, every year the deaths are played down or not mentioned at all. Even when horses have to be euthanized by the side of the track, it's hidden from viewers and spectators.

FACT
In the 2011 National, two horses died in the four-and-a-half mile steeplechase race – Ornais at the fourth jump (broken neck) and Dooneys Gate (with a broken back) at notorious Becher's Brook. The course had to be changed, to avoid people seeing the two dead horses being removed. The horse that won the race, Ballabriggs was seriously dehydrated at the end and close to collapse. Three of the top four finishing horses were so exhausted they didn't make it into the winners' enclosure.

Following the event, there were calls for the race to be banned, with one critic likening the Grand National to Spanish bullfighting.

Animal Aid director Andrew Tyler blamed the tightly packed and often high fences over a long course for making it so dangerous. "The public has been conned into believing that the Grand National is a great sporting spectacle when, in reality, it is straightforward animal abuse that is on a par with Spanish bullfighting."

TIP
The horseracing industry is a cruel one. Horses that don't make it are often destroyed. If you don't want to be part of this then don't bet on any horserace or attend one.

15. Sponsor a child abroad.
You could make the real difference to a child's life and all for a little money a day. The money raised from sponsorship goes towards not just your child's education and their future, but will also benefit the whole community.

America
If you live in America, you could sponsor a child with World Vision. In doing so, you could help bring fresh water to that child's community. Children are from a number of different countries and you get to choose who you sponsor or the site will come up with a child for you.
For details, visit - www.worldvision.org

Canada
Canada has its own organization for sponsoring children abroad. Plan is one of the oldest and largest international development agencies and they say they "are independent and inclusive of all faiths and cultures."
For details, go to http://plancanada.ca/childsponsorship

UK
For UK residents you can sponsor a child through Action Aid.

Under the scheme you can sponsor someone from a variety of countries, including Brazil, Peru, Haiti, Ethiopia, India and China amongst others.

You'll get an update on your child's progress, a picture and can also write to the child you sponsor. In certain cases, you may even be allowed to visit the child you are sponsoring, by arrangement with the charity who will make sure a support worker can go with you.
Go to www.actionaid.org.uk/102425/sponsor_a_child.html for more details.

You could also sponsor a child through Save the Children www.savethechildren.org/site/c.8rKLIXMGIpI4E/b.6146367/k.8EA1/Sponsor_A_Child.htm They need people to sponsor children in America because one in five children in the country live in poverty.

Australia
If you're thinking of sponsoring a child in Australia, visit this site for details -
http://trans.worldvision.com.au/default.aspx

TIP
Remember, there will be children in your own country needing help too. Donate unwanted clothes, food and toys to charity, including unwanted presents.

"I was shocked to learn that some airlines transport monkeys to laboratories around the world. I support the BUAV's Cargo Cruelty campaign and urge these airlines to take a compassionate stance and say no to monkey shipments."
Ricky Gervais

16. Don't fly with airlines who transport monkeys to animal research labs.

In 2011, funnyman Ricky Gervais joined *the British Union for the Abolition of Vivisection* (BUAV) **Cargo Cruelty campaign** against the shipping of monkeys by airlines to research labs. The monkeys destined for these labs are taken from the wild, or they are the offspring of those taken from the wild. They are being sent to labs in the USA, UK, Japan and Europe where they will be experimented on and usually kept in conditions that any pet owner would be prosecuted for if they did the same.

To find out more, go to www.buav.org/cargocruelty

Their site also has a list of airlines who fly monkeys to research labs and ones who don't if you go to the link and then scroll down until you see find out which airlines still transport primates for research.
Note – this list is constantly updated and you may find some airlines bow to public pressure and stop transporting monkeys.

FACT
The monkeys are placed in tiny cramped cages in cargo holds mainly on passenger flights.

TIP
If you decide not to fly with an airline because they transport monkeys to laboratories, write to them and tell them why you made that decision so that they know their policy is costing them business and their good reputation.

17. Be a good Samaritan and help others
There is a way that you can help create a more compassionate world without it costing a penny. All it takes is being nice and considerate and thinking of others.

How about –
*Taking the time to smile and say "hello" to strangers you see on the street. A friendlier world is a happier world and a happier world is a more compassionate world.

*Getting in shopping or offering to do basic tasks for an elderly or disabled person.

*When you get bad service, do you complain about it? But, when you get good service do you ever email or phone the company to say "thank you?"
Imagine how happy you would be if you worked in customer service and all you seemed to get were constant emails and phone calls of complaint and then one day you got a thank you?

*Is there a soup kitchen in your area where they feed the homeless? If so, why not ask if they need volunteers to work in it or donations of food?

*Send a care parcel to a soldier stationed abroad. Imagine what it must be like for them miles away from home and all the comforts it brings. If you're a US citizen, go to http://www.supportoursoldiers.co.uk/irshop.aspx?section=content&page=115 for info. There are also links to other sites aimed at sending parcels to personnel in other branches of the military including www.anysailor.com and www.anymarine.com
If you live in the UK, go to www.supportoursoldiers.co.uk for details. They also have a list of suggested items to include.

18. Buy dog or cat food that hasn't been tested on animals.

It may sound ridiculous, but many pet food companies test their food on lab or kennel animals. This is so they can make certain health claims like 'this food will increase your ageing dog's mobility.'

These dogs are usually kept in a lab or a kennel environment and often undergo invasive testing. It's not simply a matter of them being given the food to eat and treated like pets. And, even when they are well looked after, they are denied the right to live a normal life as companion animals and to indulge in normal behaviors.

FACT
There have been documented cases where the treatment these animals have received has fallen way short of animal welfare standards. One well-known company, debarked dogs (debarking is a veterinary surgery that involves removing tissue from the dog's vocal chords so that a dog's bark is merely a whisper), placed animals in barren cages and removed muscles from dogs' legs (they did this so they could say their food strengthened muscles).

If pet owners did the same, they'd be prosecuted.

TIP
If you want to know for certain whether a certain brand of dog or cat food is tested on lab or kenneled animals, ask the company who makes it. Ask them whether they or their suppliers use invasive tests on animals and or keep them in labs or kennels. Make them aware of the fact that there is no need to do that as pet foods can be tested on animals in their own homes under the watchful eyes of their owners. Also make them aware of the fact that you'll only buy dog food tested in the more humane way.

FACT

The US *Department of Agriculture* investigated a complaint by PETA in 2006 about invasive testing of *Procter & Gamble's IAMS* brand. This followed an undercover investigation by *PETA*, which was well documented in the press. *The USDA* agreed with PETA that the laboratory had failed to provide veterinary care and pain relief to suffering animals who were also not given sufficient space to move around in. There were 40 other violations of the federal Animal Welfare Act in total.

TIP

Be wary of pet food that makes new claims like **improves muscle tone**. To back up new claims they will have tested the food on lab animals. In the case of being able to make a claim like that the lab animal would have been fed the food for a period, then killed and dissected.

FACT

In America, the UK and the EU, *PETA* have a scheme that requires pet food companies not to directly fund lab animal testing or any tests on animals that are cruel and harmful. Go to www.peta.com (or one of the different sites listed on the home page) for details and put 'non-animal tested companion animal food' in the search box. They have a list of ethical companies who do non-invasive food testing on animals in their own homes.

FACT

In the UK, *the BUAV* used to have a *No Animal Testing Pet Food Standard*, whereby companies that didn't test their pet food on lab animals were granted their seal of approval. This no longer exists.

TIP

To find out whether the food you give your pet is not tested on lab animals, visit the *Uncaged* website at
www.uncaged.co.uk
Along with other animal protection groups, they are working to get all pet food companies to stop testing on lab animals, as this is completely unnecessary.

> *"I've learned that you shouldn't go through life with a catcher's mitt on both hands. You need to be able to throw something back."*
> Maya Angelou, baseball star.

19. Recycle don't trash.

Landfill sites are bad for the people who live near them, so try and recycle as much as possible. Recycling things like bottles and plastic ensures that there are les things lying around for animals like birds to hurt themselves on. For instance the plastic that holds together four packs van become entangled round the necks of birds and stop them feeding, so they die.

Recycling things, like paper also ensures fewer trees are chopped down that provide homes for animals like squirrels, snakes and bugs.

TIP
You can also make a little cash from recycling. Look for companies that take used clothing and textiles and aluminum cans and pay for them.

TIP
Hate your clothes, or they no longer fit? Have you considered having a clothes swapping party where you can get together with friends and pick clothes from each other's pile that suits you? Your disaster dress could be their dream outfit.

20. Get your own dog/cat neutered and encourage others to do the same.

There's one reason there's too many strays dogs and cats in rescue centers - over-breeding. The solution to this is simple - neutering or spaying.

Too many pet owners think it's unnatural to have their animals neutered or spayed, but the truth is it's that kind of thinking that leads to animals being euthanized because there's not enough people to adopt them.

TIP

Another reason for shelters being full is that stray dogs are found and they can't be traced back to their owners. That's why it's vital that you have your dog microchipped. That way, he or she will find their way back to you.

Show your pet you care and get them microchipped today.

21. If you're drinking coffee, or eating chocolate, make sure it's Fair Trade Certified.

These days, the most widely available Fairtrade products are coffee and chocolate and buying them can make a real difference to the lives of farmers and workers. Farmers are paid a good price for their products and workers earn a fair wage, meaning that your coffee and chocolate is guilt free.

TIP

Starbucks is the world's largest coffee chain and is a leader in *Fair Trade* coffee. You can buy a Fair Trade version in all their stores.

TIP

Ben & Jerry's ice cream desserts will contain just Fair Trade ingredients from 2013.

Note - They're owned by *Unilever*, a company that carries out animal experiments, but Ben & Jerry's don't use animal testing themselves.

22. Make your gardening cruelty free.
Making sure your plants stay healthy and your lawn looks good, doesn't mean killing other living things or harming the environment.

1. Rat poison tastes sweet and tasty to cats and dogs and other animals too, but if eaten it will kill them. Avoid using it completely if you can and use humane rat traps instead.

2. Ditch the weed killer and use salt on the weeds instead. It leaches into the soil and weeds won't be able to grow there any more.

3. Don't kill slugs with salt, use seaweed as a fertilizer. Slugs hate seaweed and won't go near it because of the high salt content.

4. Want to get rid of moles in your lawn? Orange peel will see them off. They hate the smell and will scurry off.

5. Grow lavender in your garden to deter ants.

6. To stop cats marking their territory on your lawn, try installing a sprinkler system that's motion activated or get some crystals that smell of citrus fruits. Cats detest the scent and will stay away. These crystals are safe around children and pets.

23. Have a charity auction or table sale.

We all have things we no longer want lying around our homes: unwanted gifts, clothes we bought in sales that no longer fit or are out of style, outdated gadgets we have no further use for?

How great would it be if you could get rid of all that clutter and turn it into bucks that you could donate to a charity of your choice?

TIP
Why not get together with friends and hold a joint sale with proceeds split between a few charities that you agree on? You could pick from type of charity, say one for a hospice, one for a children's charity and another to help a country hit by famine.

24. Don't use poison to get rid of household pests.
You don't need to use poison to get rid of those household pests. Try some natural repellants instead because they are better for you and the pests –

*Cockroaches hate bay leafs.

*Use cruelty free rat and mice traps and make sure you seal off any holes and gaps to prevent them gaining entry in the first place. *PETA* has a humane mousetrap that looks a bit like a smaller version of a hamster's cage. The mouse is caught in the trap and is then released. There are other similar traps you can buy or make yourself.

FACT

When we had mice in our house, we read a lot of nonsense by people who should know better that using humane traps was cruel because the mice wouldn't survive out in the wild and the mice would starve in the traps. Instead, these people preferred to use what I would call killing traps, where the little fellows would get caught and have their necks broken. As long as you check the humane traps regularly, they are safe to use.

*Being scared of spiders doesn't mean squashing the critters or vacuuming them up. Instead use spider traps that will lift Charlotte up and then release her outdoors. There are also sprays that are made out of natural ingredients like cloves that will make them decide to hang out elsewhere.

*If you want to stop flies getting into your home in the warm months, don't douse them in killer spray, get sprigs of lavender or lavender plants. This will see them off, as will having beaded curtains in open doorways.

FACT

Using bug sprays isn't good for you or your children and is bad for the environment. Certain cancers like bone cancer have also been linked to chemicals that are in products like bug spray and air freshener, as have respiratory problems like asthma and allergies.

25. Think about being a Samaritan or volunteer counselor.
Sometimes we just need someone to talk to about or problems; a person who will listen and not judge us. Often the best person to speak to is a complete stranger who can see situations from a neutral viewpoint.

The Samaritans operate 24-hours a day, seven-days a week and offer a number you can phone to talk to someone. You don't need to book an appointment or phone between office hours. Anything callers tell the Samaritans is completely confidential.

Could you be the person on the end of that phone, maybe helping someone who's so depressed they're thinking of taking their own life?

People can also write to them by mail or email them. Some Samaritans also allow people to drop in to discuss their problems. See your country's website for details.

FACT
Despite their name, *the Samaritans* aren't a religious organization. A British newspaper found out about the charity and dubbed them "Good Samaritans" and the name stuck.

Could you be a Samaritan?
1. Are you over 18 years of age?

2. Are you a good listener? It can be a difficult skill to master. Many of us talk too much and don't listen enough.

3. Are you easily shocked? You may hear things that you have never heard before.

4. Are you open minded and tolerant of people from all walks of life?

5. Can you listen to people without making any snap judgments?

6. Would you be able to listen to people's problems without telling people what they should do? Samaritans and counselors are there to listen, not to give people advice.

For more details of becoming a volunteer, visit your country's website.

Note – Canada and Australia don't have the Samaritans, but they will have other similar charities that need volunteer counselors. Why not volunteer?

America
In America, the Samaritans are called **Samaritans USA** and they have professional and volunteer-run public education programs, as well as hotlines people can phone for help.
For more details, visit www.samaritansusa.org

TIP
There are also what's known as suicide prevention hotlines that need volunteers. To find them visit the www.befrienders.org home page and just below the menu bar go to "find a Helpline by country" and select the country you are in. Often these hotlines are short of volunteers, especially around Christmas time and Thanksgiving when people are particularly prone to depression.

UK & Republic of Ireland
Their site has a find you nearest branch function on the home page. Visit www.samaritans.org
To find out how to volunteer, go to your nearest branch.

FACT
In the UK, the Samaritans get 5 million calls a year. They are contacted every 6 seconds.

TIP

Some Samaritans hold information sessions for potential volunteers. Why not attend one and decide if you could help?

TIP

Many colleges and schools have volunteer counselors (often called outreach counselors) who will speak to students who are experiencing problems like bullying and peer pressure. These counselors are usually students themselves who live on campus.

TIP

If you don't live in the USA, the UK or Ireland and want details of your nearest hotline (helpline), visit www.befrienders.org
If you phone up or email and ask about volunteering, someone will help you.

"Change is not made without inconvenience."
Samuel Johnson

Chapter 9
Become a cruelty free crusader

At times, it may seem like there is nothing we can do that can even make a dent in the cruelty in this world, whether its people forced into slave labor or animals being immobilized so they can have poison dripped into their eyes. But the truth is we all have more power than we realize.

You see, companies want your money. They want you to buy their products. And, if enough people won't buy from them because they use practices the public considers unacceptable and those non-buyers make it clear exactly why they won't buy, these companies will change their ways. Companies do care about what consumers think when it costs them cash.

Stay informed.
To know how companies conduct their business, we need to stay informed. Being informed is the key to being a cruelty free crusader.

If you want to know about companies who don't use cruelty free practices as well as those that do, you need to keep updated. As well as the organizations mentioned in other chapters, here are a few organizations that can help.

Note – Most of those listed are aimed at helping the rights of workers as animal welfare charities have already been covered in previous chapters.

Clean Clothes Campaign (CCC) Their aim is to improve the working conditions of garment workers throughout the world. They do this by trying to make sure that consumers like you are kept informed. They are based in Europe, but they also work with similar organizations in the USA, Canada and Australia. Read more about them and their campaigns at www.cleanclothes.org

Labor Behind the Label also support the rights of garment workers and aims to improve the working conditions of all workers by publicizing their cause, pressurizing companies who use labor into making sure workers are treated fairly, supporting workers as they battle for decent pay and conditions, as well as campaigning to get governments to ensure better treatment for workers. Read more at www.labourbehindthelabel.org

www.change.org describes itself as an "online activism platform for social change that raises awareness about important causes and connects people to opportunities for powerful action." You can use their site to organize you own campaign and set up a petition.

Previous campaigns include helping to get Chinese dissident artist Ai Weiwei out of prison, getting Hilary Clinton to support the women's right to driver campaign in Saudi Arabia (women were banned from driving in the country) and the toughening up of animal cruelty laws in Canada prompted by 100 sled dogs being brutally killed in British Columbia. They have a number of causes on their site, ranging from animals, human rights and gay rights to woman's rights and human trafficking.

Greenpeace want to save the planet. Read more about them and their campaigns at www.greenpeace.org/international/en

Although they are based in the UK, Oxfam are a global organization. Go to www.oxfam.org.uk to hear about the work they are doing and their current campaigns.

The Born Free Foundation is a worldwide animal conservation charity whose aims are to stop individual animal suffering and to protect endangered species in the wild. Visit www.bornfree.org.uk to see their current campaigns.

TIP
If you're on Facebook, Twitter or any other social networking site, follow, friend or like the organizations on them.

TIP
Are you a sports fan? Ask your favorite club what they do to ensure that official merchandise is made by workers who are treated fairly. Sportswear is one area where workers can be exploited.

Use technology to keep other people informed.
Technology is the cruelty free crusaders friend. If there was no Internet how many people would you tell if you found out that something you were about to buy was made using slave labor or tested on animals? Half a dozen. Maybe?

The good thing about the Internet, is that if you it has never been so easy to get your message across. Using social media like Facebook and Twitter, as well as blogs and message boards is the key.

Say you tweet about a product to 600 of your followers on Twitter. Then a few of those people read your tweet and decide to retweet it. Add all the people together who have read what you've had to say and your audience could run into the thousands.

TIP

You could also start a Facebook page or group and see if you can attract anyone else who feels like you do. Use a name that makes your cause clear i.e. **AXE CHILD LABOR, LIVE CRUELTY FREE, STOP TESTING COSMETICS ON ANIMALS** or **BAN SWEATSHOPS**.

Start a petition

There are also petition sites where you can upload a petition, say asking for a company not to sell fur or to make sure their workers are paid fairly.

Petition sites –

http://www.38degrees.org.uk brings people together to start petitions. 15 millions people so far have done just that. Previous petitions include, one to improve conditions in puppy and cat farms and one to get chain store Matalan to reveal how much money they paid in compensations to victims of a factory collapse where workers made their clothes. The site is UK based.

www.ipetitions.com has attracted millions of signatures on a variety of topics.

Watch out for petition sites that offer to pay you a small fee for every signature. Those sites are aimed at collecting names and emails for spammers and go against the spirit of petitions, namely to express your views and not to cash in.

Petition tips –

1. When writing an online petition its best if you are short and to the point. Look at other petitions to see how it's done.

2. Petitions must have an aim i.e. "the undersigned want current laws changed so that non-essential animal testing will be banned."

3. You don't need to be emotional as the facts should speak for themselves.

4. You can add links to information in your petition, so people can read about the facts themselves.

5. Allow everyone who signs to be anonymous if they want to be. This will dispel their fears that you may be just trying to get their details to sell onto spammers.

6. Post links to the petition on your website, blog, Twitter, Facebook and any other networks you use. You need to get the word out. You can also use the link to the petition as your signature in an email. Make sure it's your personal one though and not your work as your employers may object. You can also create a badge on Facebook.

TIP
Don't forget to send a tweet or message to the company themselves. Let them know what potential customers like you think. Companies have no way of knowing people's thoughts unless people tell them.

"Unless someone like you cares a whole awful lot, nothing is going to get better. It's not."
Dr. Seuss

Express your views
You've just watched a documentary exposing a store that you shop in as one that uses underpaid labor. You're shocked you always thought it was a pretty good store. How do you let the company know how you feel about their lack of ethics?

*Write a letter to their HQ. Try and get a named person to send it to so it doesn't get lost. This should be someone like the managing director, chief executive or a director.
Write to newspaper and magazine letter pages telling them what you think.

*Start your own petition and collect as many signatures as you can and either send it in or go along with a group of friends. Try and get your local newspaper to cover you presenting the petition. You may have to make an appointment with the company beforehand.

*Send an email detailing your concerns. No personal abuse.

*Go into the store and tell one of the shopping assistants how you feel. Remember though, they only work there, so be polite.

TIP
Whether a letter or in an email, the best sort of communication, are the ones that start something like "as a lifelong shopper in your store/buyer of your products, I was upset to find out that…" If you want companies to act more responsibly towards human beings and animals, you need to make them think that they will be losing valuable customers like you if they don't change their ways.

Bottom line – companies care about making money that's all. If they think they will lose money they will change the way they operate to maintain their profits.

TIP
It may also help if you say that you have heard a rival company is more ethical and you will shop there from now on. Companies hate the thought of losing customers to their rivals.

Attend a peaceful protest

Did you know that there are countries where the government and companies can do whatever they want, yet people aren't allowed to protest?

If you're lucky enough to live in America, Canada, Australia or the UK, the good news is that you are allowed to protest as long as you abide by the law.

Friends of the Earth have a free PDF document called "**How to protest on the right side of the law in the UK**." Not only does the document offer advice on how to stay on the right side of the law, there's also tips on how make sure your protest has the right kind of impact
www.foe.co.uk/resource/how_tos/cyw_59_protest_law.pdf

How to organize a peaceful protest

The key to any successful protest is organization.

Here are some tips –
*Check with the police and your local council to find out if you need some kind of permit or permission to have the protest.

*Decide beforehand what you want to say. What is your message? This could be that you want people to boycott a certain store because they sell something like sandblasted jeans (workers in the factories that make them have died because they've ingested the silicon used to give them that sand blasted effect), fur or Foie gras. If you get stuck think 'what is my objective/aim or what do I want to achieve?

*Decide beforehand what kind of protest it's going to be and where it will take place. Will you protest outside a store or an organization? Will you protest in a town square or outside a shopping mall (centre)? Will it be silent protest or will there be chants?

*Discuss what you'll do if the protest gets out of hand as some protests do attract troublemakers. For that reason, try wherever possible to only include people you or your friends know in the protest.

*Make up leaflets so that if people want to know why you are protesting you have something to give them. Who knows, they may even join the protest.

*Arrange a meet up place for everyone involved. That way you don't end up with confusion.

*Publicize the protest. Use local newspapers, cable stations and radio stations, use social networking like Facebook (maybe set up a page or group) and Twitter. The more people who know the more people who might turn up. Also try and write in to local newspapers and radio and cable channels too. Maybe they will be interested in interviewing you?

*Make up banners and posters to take with you. Make the message as short and clear as possible. For instance, NO TO ANIMAL TESTING or NO TO USING CHILD LABOR.

*Make sure that everyone knows this is a peaceful protest and that participants shouldn't behave in a threatening or confrontational way.

*Could you line up a celebrity or high profile supporter to speak at the protest? This will get the media interested in your protest.

TIP

Protests should be carried out on public land wherever possible. If you protest on private land you may get arrested for trespass.

TIP

If a store security guard asks you to move away, you should ask where the store's land ends, because you have the right to protest on the public highway.

TIP

Be careful that your behavior or that of any of the protestors doesn't cross the line and become a criminal offence. This could mean harassing someone by making them feel threatened by you or your presence or by trying to get them to do something they don't want to do.

FACT

It was protests by the Suffragette movement that led to women getting the vote in the UK.

Other things you can do -

1. If a company doesn't sell a certain cruelty free product, say make up that's not tested on animals or Fair Trade coffee, ask for it. Get your friends to ask for it. The more people who ask the more likely stores are to stock it.

2. Shop in stores that sell Fair Trade goods. Things like Fair Trade coffee and bananas are widely available. The more people who buy them the greater the demand, and the more farmers and workers there will be who are paid a fair wage for their produce.

3. Ask stores why their clothing is so cheap. Who makes the garments and how do they make sure no child labor or slave labor is used? Where are the clothes made? Do they have any literature showing workers making them?

Useful Websites

The following websites are a good source of information for those looking to live a more compassionate life. They cover a variety of things like buying Fair Trade and cosmetics that aren't tested on animals

Note – their inclusion here is in no way an endorsement of the site and its contents. Sites are listed for guidance only.

Animal charities

www.aspca.org
The American Society for the Prevention of Cruelty to Animals

www.animalaid.org.uk
Animal Aid are based in the UK. They highlight the plight of animals, including in cruel sports like horseracing and pheasant shooting.

www.awlnsw.com.au
Animal Welfare League New South Wales. As well as campaigning on behalf of animals in Australia, they also has cats and dogs needing new homes.

www.spcamontreal.com
The Canadian Society for the Prevention of Cruelty to Animals (CSPCA) was the first humane society in Canada and was founded in 1869.

www.dogstrust.org
Dogs Trust (UK) never put a healthy dog down.

www.humanesociety.org
The Humane Society of the United States

www.peta.org/index_landing.asp
PETA (people for the Ethical Treatment of Animals) operate worldwide.

www.petrescue.com.au
Pet Rescue tries to find homes for unwanted pets in Australia.

www.rspca.org.uk/freedomfood
The Royal Society for the Protection of Cruelty to Animals run the **Freedom Food scheme** in the UK.

www.viva.org.uk
Viva (Vegetarians International Voice for Animals)

Anti-vivisection organizations
Note – vivisection means experimenting on live animals.

www.aavs.org
American Anti-vivisection Society (AAVS)

www.ad-international.org
Animal Defenders International, are a global organization who also campaign to replace animal experiments.

http://animal-lib.org.au
Animal Liberation has branches in all states of Australia and many thousands of supporters.

www.buav.org
The British Union for the Abolition of Vivisection (BUAV)

www.drhadwentrust.org
Not only do they campaign against animal experiments, they actively fund alternatives.

www.four-paws.org.uk
Four Paws work to end all animal suffering and help all creatures great and small.

www.navs.org.uk
The National Anti-Vivisection Society, are one of the oldest anti-vivisection organizations in the world.

www.uncaged.co.uk
Exposing animal cruelty, especially in labs.

http://vivisectionresearch.ca
They campaign against vivisection in Canada.

Children's Charities

www.loveourchildrenusa.org
This American charity wants to end violence against children whether they are being bullied or assaulted by their own parents.

www.barnardos.org.au
www.barnardos.org.uk
Barnados have projects that help children all over the world.

www.childrensdefense.org
The US-based *Child's Defense Fund* motto is "leave no child behind."

www.oxfam.org.uk
Oxfam are based in the UK, but the work they do helps the poorest children in the world.

www.savethechildren.org.uk
www.savethechildren.org.au

www.savethechildren.ca

Save The Children, are based in the UK but they help children throughout the world. They have websites in the UK, Australia and Canada.

Save the Children also run a program where you can sponsor a child in the USA -

www.savethechildren.org/site/c.8rKLIXMGIpI4E/b.6153159/
k.C8D5/USA.htm

www.soschildrensvillages.ca

SOS Children's Villages Canada, take care of children who've been orphaned or abandoned.

Cruelty Free Cosmetics & toiletries

There are more companies than ever before offering cosmetics and toiletries, where neither the ingredients nor the final products, are tested on animals. It would take up too much space to list them, but these are the most reliable sites.

www.gocrueltyfree.org

The Leaping Bunny List allows you to search by product and country.

www.choosecrueltyfree.org.au

The number one site for Australians who want to go cruelty free.

www.aavs.org

To get to the **Compassionate Shopping Guide** on *the American Anti-Vivisection Society* site, go to the home page and click on **Shop with compassion** on the top right hand side of the page.

www.vegansociety.com/afssearch.aspx?ad=677814

The Vegan Society does an **Animal free shopper guide**.

Fair Trade

Buying Fair Trade makes a real difference to people's lives.

www.fta.org.au
Fairtrade site for Australia and New Zealand

www.fairtrade.org.uk
Home of Fairtrade in the UK

http://fairtrade.ca
Fair Trade Canada

http://fairtradeusa.org/
Website for *the Fair Trade Certification in the USA*

Note – In the UK, Australia and New Zealand it's called *Fairtrade*. In Canada and the USA, it's called *Fair Trade* although they are the same thing.

www.ethicalconsumer.org/home.aspx
Site offering tips on how to be a more ethical shopper.

Human Rights Charities

www.amnesty.org
Amnesty International are probably the most famous organization of its type in the world.

www.actionaid.org.uk/100084/other_actionaid_websites.html
Action Aid has one aim: to end poverty wherever it may be. They offer sponsor a child schemes and do various famine appeals. Go to the link to visit their various countries' sites.

www.cartercenter.org

The Carter Center promotes human rights throughout the world and is based in Atlanta in the USA.

www.hrw.org

Human Rights Watch highlight human rights abuses all over the world.

www.msf.org

Medecins Sans Frontieres (it's French and translates as doctors without borders) is an international humanitarian aid organization. They provide emergency medical assistance to populations in danger, in several countries throughout the world.

Vegetarian & Vegan Organizations
If you're planning to eat less meat or to go vegetarian or even vegan, these sites offer free advice.

www.ivu.org
International Vegetarian Union (IVU)

www.navs-online.org
North American Vegetarian Society (NAVS)

www.vegansociety.com
The Vegan Society

www.vegsoc.org

The Vegetarian Society (UK) allows companies to put their logo on products that are suitable for vegetarians (subject to checks).

www.viva.org.uk

Vegetarians International Voice for Animals (Viva!)

www.vegetarian.org.uk
The Vegetarian & Vegan Foundation

Book List

Animal Liberation: The Definitive Classic of the Animal Movement
by Peter Singer, Published by Harper
ISBN- 978-0061711305

Giving: How Each of Us Can Change the World
by Bill Clinton, Published by Knopf
ISBN- 978-1615568093

How to be an Ethical Shopper: The Practical Guide to Buying What You Believe in
by Melissa Corkhill, Published by Impact Publishing Ltd
ISBN- 978-1904601456

How to Cook Everything Vegetarian: Simple Meatless Recipes for Great Food
by Mark Bittman, Published by John Wiley & Sons
ISBN- 978-0764524837

Random Acts of Kindness
by The Editors of Conari Press, Published by Conari Press
ISBN-13: 978-1573248532

Skinny Bitch
by Rory Freedman & Kim Barnouin, Published by Running Press
ISBN- 978-0762424931

The Better World Shopping Guide: Every Dollar Makes a Difference (Better World Shopping Guide: Every Dollar Can Make a Difference)
by Ellis Jones, Published by New Society Publishers
ISBN- 978-0865716803

The Good Deed Guide: Simple Ways to Make the World a Better Place
by James Grace, Lisa Grace, Published by Quirk Books
ISBN-13: 978-1931686334

The Kind Diet: A Simple Guide to Feeling Great, Losing Weight, and Saving the Planet
by Alicia Silverstone, Published by Rodale
ISBN- 978-1609611354

Volunteering: The Ultimate Teen Guide (It Happened To Me)
By Kathlyn Gray, Published by Scarecrow Press
ISBN- 978-0810858336

Printed in Great Britain
by Amazon.co.uk, Ltd.,
Marston Gate.